How to Make Money with AI

David Moore

Published by David Moore, 2025.

HOW TO MAKE MONEY WITH AI

First edition. June 1, 2025.

ISBN: 979-8231436804

Written by David Moore.

Table of Contents

To the dreamers, the doers, and the disruptors—may this book give you the clarity and confidence to build your future with AI.

"The future is already here—it's just not evenly distributed."—William Gibson

Chapter 1: Welcome to the AI Gold Rush

A New Frontier of Wealth

We are living through one of the most profound technological shifts in human history—and most people don't even realize it yet. Artificial Intelligence isn't just changing how we write, design, sell, and communicate. It's transforming **how we make money.**

In the past, wealth was tied to land, factories, or insider access. Today, it's tied to **knowledge, speed, and digital leverage**. Those who understand AI—and how to apply it—are stepping into opportunities that didn't exist even five years ago. From solo creators automating entire businesses to full-time workers launching AI side hustles, the game has changed.

And you don't need to be a tech genius to play it.

Why This Book Exists

This book isn't about theory. It's about **actionable steps**. Each chapter gives you real-world strategies to tap into AI tools and models to:

- Build income streams
- Serve clients faster
- Launch digital products
- Scale without burnout
- Stay ahead of the curve

Whether you're a freelancer, entrepreneur, full-time employee, or total beginner, you'll find **systems, business models, and tools** you can start using today—even if you've never written a line of code in your life.

The AI Advantage

Here's why AI is the biggest money-making opportunity of our generation:

- **Speed**: What took hours now takes minutes—or seconds.

- **Scale**: You can serve 10 or 10,000 people with the same effort.

- **Automation**: You don't have to trade time for money anymore.

- **Access**: The tools are free or cheap, and the learning curve is dropping.

It's not about replacing humans. It's about **supercharging what you can do** with the right mindset and tools.

A Word of Caution

Yes, AI can be a powerful ally—but it's not magic. You still need:

- **Critical thinking** to spot opportunity

- **Ethical awareness** to use it responsibly

- **Consistency** to actually get results

The people winning in this space aren't always the smartest. They're the most **curious**, **adaptable**, and **willing to experiment.**

Your Journey Starts Now

In the coming chapters, we'll explore dozens of AI-powered income strategies—from freelancing and automation to product creation and investing. Each section will offer:

- What you need to get started
- Tools to use (free and paid)
- Realistic income potential
- Tips to stand out in a growing crowd

This is not a "get rich quick" book. But if you're willing to learn and take action, you'll have a **roadmap to turn AI into income**—on your terms.

Let's begin.

◈ Reflection & Action: Chapter 1 – Welcome to the AI Gold Rush

Reflect:

1. What excites you most about the possibilities of making money with AI?
2. What limiting beliefs (if any) do you currently hold about your ability to succeed with tech or digital income?
3. Do you see yourself more as a creator, a helper, a builder, or an investor? Why?

Journal Prompt:

"If I could use AI to replace just one stressful or time-consuming part of my work or life, it would be..."

Take Action:

◈ 1. Choose Your Focus:

Write down which of the following paths feels most aligned with your goals:

- Freelance services using AI
- Content creation and automation
- Product development (apps, courses, etc.)
- AI-enhanced investing
- Passive digital income (ebooks, art, affiliate)

◈ 2. Get Familiar with Tools:

Pick **one AI tool** to explore today. Some beginner-friendly suggestions:

- **ChatGPT** (for content, copywriting, planning)
- **Canva with AI features** (for design work)
- **Leonardo.Ai or Midjourney** (for art generation)
- **Tome or Notion AI** (for organizing ideas)

◈ 3. Set a Goal:

Write down a **1-month outcome**:

"In the next 30 days, I will use AI to ______ and make at least $__."

Power Quote:

"Opportunities are like sunrises. If you wait too long, you miss them."
— William Arthur Ward

Chapter 2: Understanding Artificial Intelligence

What Is AI—Really?

Let's strip away the buzzwords. At its core, **artificial intelligence** is a system or machine that mimics human intelligence to perform tasks. These tasks include learning, problem-solving, pattern recognition, and even creativity. Unlike regular software that needs to be explicitly told what to do, AI can analyze data, make decisions, and improve over time.

In short: **AI helps you do things faster, smarter, and—sometimes—better.**

There are different types of AI, but for the purpose of making money, we'll focus on the most accessible and monetizable forms.

The Key Types of AI You Can Profit From

1. Generative AI

This is the AI you've probably heard the most about. It creates new content—like text, images, or video—based on prompts or training data.

- **Text-based**: ChatGPT, Claude, Gemini (for writing, emails, code, scripts)
- **Image-based**: Midjourney, DALL·E, Leonardo.Ai (for art, book covers, ads)
- **Audio/video**: ElevenLabs, Synthesia, Pictory (for voiceovers, avatars, clips)

2. Predictive AI

This type analyzes historical data to make forecasts or recommendations.

- Used in finance, marketing, e-commerce, and even sports betting.
- It powers tools like stock prediction platforms and ad performance optimizers.

3. Automation AI

This category includes AI that replaces repetitive human tasks through scripts, bots, or workflows.

- Examples: customer support bots, AI email responders, automated lead generation
- Tools: Zapier + OpenAI, ManyChat, Tidio, Jasper Workflows

The Building Blocks: How AI Works (In Simple Terms)

Most modern AI models are built using **machine learning**, where computers are trained on massive datasets to identify patterns. For example, a language model like ChatGPT was trained on huge amounts of text data so it can "understand" and generate human-like language.

Other essential elements include:

- **Data:** The fuel AI needs to function. The more, the better.

- **Algorithms**: The rules or methods that guide how the AI learns.
- **Models**: Pretrained structures like GPT-4 that you can use instantly.

You don't need to build models yourself. You just need to **know how to use them effectively**.

Why This Matters for Making Money

You don't need to understand the math behind AI to profit from it.

But you do need to understand what AI *can* do—because:

- It helps you pick the right tools for the job.
- It lets you talk confidently to clients or partners.
- It prevents you from wasting time or falling for hype.

Think of AI as a **power tool**. You don't need to know how a drill works inside—just how to use it to build something amazing.

AI Is Not Magic—It's Leverage

The best way to think about AI? **Leverage.**

It helps you:

- Do more with less time
- Produce content faster than competitors
- Test business ideas without heavy investment

- Offer higher-value services as a solo entrepreneur
- Create digital products that scale infinitely

Those who **learn how to work with AI**, not against it, will own the future.

◈ Reflection & Action: Chapter 2 – Understanding Artificial Intelligence

Reflect:

1. Which type of AI (generative, predictive, automation) are you most interested in—and why?
2. How could AI help eliminate a task you currently find repetitive, time-consuming, or expensive?
3. What is one fear or hesitation you have about using AI, and how can you begin to overcome it?

Journal Prompt:
"If I treated AI like my business partner, what role would I assign it today?"

Take Action:
◈ **1. Explore One AI Tool Today**
Pick a tool from this list and spend 15 minutes testing it:

- **ChatGPT** → for writing, brainstorming, and outlines
- **Leonardo.Ai** or **DALL·E** → for generating images/art
- **ElevenLabs** → to turn text into lifelike voiceovers
- **Tome.app** → for fast pitch decks or slide presentations

◈ 2. List 3 Problems AI Could Help You Solve

Think about challenges in your work or personal life. For each one, jot down how AI could assist:

- Example: "I hate writing blog posts" → Use ChatGPT to create a content calendar and rough drafts.

◈ 3. Watch a Tutorial

Search YouTube or TikTok for "how to use [AI tool] for beginners" and watch just **one short video** to get visual guidance.

Power Quote:
"AI won't replace you—but someone using AI will."
— Unknown

Chapter 3: The AI Economy

A Global Shift You Can't Ignore

The global economy is shifting—and fast. Artificial Intelligence isn't just a technological innovation; it's an **economic earthquake** that's redefining how industries operate, how labor is valued, and how money flows. Those who recognize this early will have a powerful advantage.

In the 1990s, the internet created millionaires. In the 2010s, mobile apps did the same. **Now, it's AI's turn.**

But while most people worry about job loss or change, smart entrepreneurs are asking a different question:

"Where is the money flowing, and how can I position myself to catch it?"

The Main Drivers of the AI Economy

1. **Automation of Repetitive Labor**
   AI is replacing or assisting with customer support, data entry, scheduling, transcription, basic research, and even legal and medical review. This creates space for **leaner teams** and **outsourced services**—which you can provide using AI.
2. **Faster Content Production**
   From newsrooms to e-commerce stores, content is king. AI tools like ChatGPT, Jasper, and Canva's Magic Write are letting solo creators do the work of entire teams. This fuels demand for:

- Blog writers
- Script generators

- SEO experts
- Newsletter creators
- Product description writers

1. **New Business Models**
   AI has birthed brand-new ways of earning, including:

- **Prompt engineering services**
- **AI-generated product stores**
- **AI-assisted course creation**
- **Niche SaaS tools powered by OpenAI**

1. **Mass Personalization**
   AI allows businesses to personalize marketing, emails, recommendations, and offers at scale. This creates huge demand for **AI-powered marketing freelancers**, **automation consultants**, and **data analysts**.

Where the Money Is

Let's break it down:

Area	Opportunity	What You Need
E-commerce	AI-generated designs, product descriptions, chatbots	Midjourney, Shopify, Copy.ai
Digital Products	Ebooks, templates, guides created with AI	Canva, ChatGPT, Gumroad
Freelancing	Writing, editing, SEO, email marketing	Upwork, Jasper, Notion AI
Investing	AI-powered research, stock/ crypto bots	Finchat, Tradytics, CryptoHopper
Education	Online courses created or enhanced by AI	Teachable, Synthesia, ChatGPT
SaaS Tools	Simple AI-powered web apps	Bubble.io, Zapier, OpenAI API

In all these areas, **speed and uniqueness** are your advantages. If you can deliver quickly, or in a way that feels new or personalized, you're already ahead of the curve.

Big Players, Big Moves

Major corporations are pouring billions into AI development:

- **Microsoft** invested heavily in OpenAI (makers of ChatGPT).
- **Google** launched Gemini and integrated AI into Docs, Gmail, and Search.
- **Meta** (Facebook) is experimenting with AI across social media and ads.
- **Amazon** uses AI in logistics, customer experience, and Alexa.

Why should you care? Because **where big money goes, opportunity follows.**

You don't need to be a tech giant to benefit—you just need to position yourself at the **edges of innovation**, where tools are accessible and nimble entrepreneurs can move fast.

You're Not Too Late

People often ask, "Did I miss the boat?"

No. You're right on time—**if you start now**. Most people are still watching from the sidelines, uncertain and overwhelmed.

You? You're reading this. You're learning. You're getting ready to act.

That puts you ahead of 95% of the world.

◈ Reflection & Action: Chapter 3 – The AI Economy

Reflect:

1. Which industry or opportunity mentioned in this chapter interests you the most? Why?
2. How is your current job, skill set, or business affected by the rise of AI?
3. What's one specific way you could apply AI to increase income or save time in your current work?

Journal Prompt:

"The area of the AI economy where I see the biggest opportunity for myself is..."

Take Action:

◈ 1. Choose a Niche to Explore

Pick **one money-making area** from the table below to dive into this week:

- E-commerce
- Digital products
- Freelancing
- Investing
- Online education
- SaaS tools

◈ 2. Identify 3 Tools Used in That Niche
Search for the most common AI tools in your chosen field. Write them down and test at least one.

◈ 3. Create a Quick Test Project
For example:

- Write a blog post using ChatGPT
- Generate a product mockup with Midjourney
- Create a mini-course outline using AI
- Use an AI stock scanner to review today's market

Don't aim for perfection—aim to **take action** and learn.

Power Quote:
"The best way to predict the future is to create it."
— Peter Drucker

Chapter 4: Myths and Realities of AI Income

The Truth Behind the Hype

If you've spent any time on YouTube or social media, you've likely seen flashy headlines like:

- "Make $10,000 a month with ChatGPT!"
- "AI Millionaire in 30 Days!"
- "This one prompt changed my life!"

It's easy to get swept up in the excitement—but let's pause. Because if you're serious about building long-term, sustainable income with AI, you need to see **through the hype** and understand what's real, what's exaggerated, and what actually works.

This chapter is about **grounding your expectations** so you can build smarter, faster, and with less frustration.

Myth #1: AI Will Make You Rich Overnight

Reality: AI can accelerate your progress—but it won't skip the process.

Yes, you can launch a business or side hustle faster than ever. But no tool replaces discipline, experimentation, or marketing. Think of AI as **a turbocharger**, not a lottery ticket.

Success still requires:

- A clear value proposition
- Knowing your target audience

- Offering something people actually need
- Showing up consistently

Myth #2: You Have to Be a Programmer

Reality: Most money-making opportunities with AI require **no coding at all.**

Platforms like ChatGPT, Canva, Notion AI, and Pictory are designed for regular users. Tools like Zapier, Make.com, and Bubble let you build apps, workflows, and systems visually.

You don't need to build AI—you just need to **build with AI.**

Myth #3: Everyone's Already Doing It

Reality: Most people are still clueless about how to use AI effectively.

Yes, AI is everywhere in the media. But in reality:

- Most businesses haven't integrated it yet.
- Most freelancers don't use it to improve delivery.
- Most creators haven't scratched the surface of automation.

That means **huge opportunity** if you get in now and specialize.

Myth #4: AI Will Take All the Jobs

Reality: AI will change jobs—but it will also **create new roles.**

Think about it:

- Who trains and manages AI systems?

- Who creates content to teach others about AI?
- Who connects clients with AI-powered solutions?

There will be demand for **AI-savvy freelancers**, **consultants**, **creators**, and **tool builders**—especially those who blend human skills (empathy, creativity, judgment) with tech.

Myth #5: AI Is Just a Fad

Reality: AI is already embedded in everything—from phones to hospitals to marketing. It's not a trend—**it's a tectonic shift.**

We're at the same stage as the early internet. Skeptics dismissed email and ecommerce too. Then Amazon happened. Then Google. Then Facebook. Now, it's AI's turn.

This is your moment to **build, test, and grow** while the tools are cheap, the field is wide open, and curiosity is your superpower.

The Bottom Line

AI isn't a magic wand. But it's also not a gimmick. It's a tool. A powerful one.

You can use it to:

- Launch your first side hustle
- Double your freelance output
- Build content faster
- Solve real problems for real people

You just need the right mindset, strategy, and follow-through.

◈ Reflection & Action: Chapter 4 – Myths and Realities of AI Income

Reflect:

1. Which myth about AI income have you personally believed before reading this chapter?
2. What surprised you about the actual realities of earning money with AI?
3. How can adjusting your expectations now help you avoid burnout or disappointment later?

Journal Prompt:
_"I used to believe _______ about making money with AI, but now I understand ______."

Take Action:

◈ 1. Reframe Your Mindset

Write down three **realistic truths** to guide your AI income journey:

- AI won't do the work for me—it will do it **with** me.
- I don't need to be an expert, just **one step ahead.**
- Progress over perfection will win every time.

◈ 2. Identify Your Strengths

Make a quick list of 3 personal skills or interests you can **combine with AI** to build income:

- Writing, design, teaching, marketing, problem-solving, etc.

◈ 3. Spot a Real Opportunity

Scroll through Fiverr, Upwork, or Gumroad. Find **one AI-related service** or product someone is offering successfully.

Ask:

- Can I do this too?
- Can I do it better, faster, or with a unique angle?

◈ **Bonus:** Screenshot it. Save it as inspiration.

Power Quote:

"The people who win are the ones who stick around after the hype dies down."

— David Moore

Chapter 5: The Mindset for AI Entrepreneurship

Tools Are Only Half the Battle

You've now seen how AI works, where the money flows, and what's real versus hype. But none of that will matter if your **mindset isn't aligned** with this new economy.

We're not just entering an era of automation—we're entering an era that rewards creativity, experimentation, and fast implementation. And the people who succeed with AI aren't necessarily tech geniuses. They're **resilient, curious, and relentless.**

Let's talk about the mindset it takes to win.

1. Adopt an Explorer's Mentality

The AI space is evolving daily. New tools drop. Old ones update. Use cases shift.

You don't need to master everything—you need to **stay curious.**

Successful AI entrepreneurs don't wait for permission. They:

- Click every button
- Try every setting
- Break stuff and learn

They explore not because they have all the answers, but because they **know the answers are out there.**

2. Focus on Use, Not Just Knowledge

Don't get stuck in endless learning loops. There's a difference between:

- **Learning AI**
- and **using AI to solve real problems**

The people making money aren't the ones watching YouTube tutorials for hours—they're the ones who open a tool, mess with it, and figure out how to deliver value.

Action is the best teacher in the AI world.

3. Start Small—But Start Now

You don't need to launch a six-figure AI agency overnight. You need:

- One small win
- One satisfied client
- One digital product
- One test campaign

Stack enough of those "small wins" and they become big ones. The key is to get in motion—even if it's messy, even if it's awkward.

Progress beats perfection. Every. Single. Time.

4. Think Like a Problem Solver

AI is just a toolbox. What matters is your ability to look at a person, business, or market and ask:

"How can I solve a problem here faster, better, or cheaper using AI?"

This mindset will:

- Make you irreplaceable as a freelancer
- Help you stand out from low-effort competitors
- Unlock product and service ideas no one else sees

Remember: People don't pay for AI. They pay for **outcomes**.

5. Embrace Rapid Reinvention

This isn't a once-and-done economy. The AI space moves fast—and you'll need to move with it.

That means:

- Being okay with pivoting
- Not tying your identity to one product or platform
- Reinventing your offers when needed

The winners aren't rigid. They're adaptable. When something stops working, they don't panic. They iterate.

The Entrepreneur's Edge

In a world full of spectators, you're choosing to be a **participant**.

- You're testing ideas.
- You're solving problems.

- You're building income on your terms.

The mindset you bring into this journey is your most valuable asset—**more than tools, money, or even experience.**

◈ Reflection & Action: Chapter 5 – The Mindset for AI Entrepreneurship

Reflect:

1. Do you currently think like an explorer—or are you waiting for things to be perfect before starting?
2. What "small win" could you aim for this week to get momentum going?
3. Are there any beliefs or habits you need to let go of to thrive in the fast-moving AI world?

Journal Prompt:
"If I fully believed I could succeed with AI, the first thing I'd do is..."

Take Action:
◈ 1. Pick a Micro-Mission
Choose a tiny, low-risk task to complete this week using AI:

- Write a blog intro with ChatGPT
- Generate a T-shirt design in Midjourney
- Make a one-minute voiceover using ElevenLabs
- Build a quick automation using Zapier

◈ 2. Track One Win per Day

For the next 3 days, write down one action you took—even if it's small. This builds consistency and confidence.

◈ 3. Set a "No-Quit" Rule

Decide right now:

"For the next 30 days, I will explore AI tools and income ideas with curiosity and commitment. I don't have to be perfect. I just have to keep going."

Print that. Tape it to your wall. Live it.

Power Quote:

"You don't rise to the level of your goals. You fall to the level of your systems."

— James Clear

Chapter 6: Making Money with ChatGPT and Other LLMs

The Power of Large Language Models (LLMs)

By now, you've likely heard the name **ChatGPT**—or maybe you've used it. But what you may not fully realize is this:

ChatGPT isn't just a chatbot—it's a money-making machine in the right hands.

ChatGPT and other large language models (LLMs) like Claude, Gemini, and Meta's LLaMA are capable of writing, brainstorming, coding, researching, translating, and more. And while most people use it to save time, smart entrepreneurs use it to **create value—and get paid for it.**

Let's break down how.

What Can You Do with ChatGPT?

1. Write for Others

- Blog posts
- Newsletters
- Product descriptions
- SEO content
- LinkedIn profiles

2. Create Digital Products

- Ebooks

- Templates
- Course outlines
- Lead magnets
- Workbooks

3. Offer Freelance Services

- Cold emails
- Sales scripts
- Resume optimization
- Business plans
- Social media captions

4. Build Tools or Systems

- Chatbots
- Customer support scripts
- Idea generators
- Form-fillers
- Email automations

5. Teach or Train Others

- AI coaching or tutorials

- Workshops for small businesses
- "Done-for-you" prompt packs

Real-World Monetization Models

Model	What You Sell	Who Pays You
Freelancer	Content created with ChatGPT	Clients via Fiverr, Upwork, LinkedIn
Product Creator	Ebooks, scripts, prompt bundles	Customers via Gumroad, Etsy, Payhip
Coach/ Consultant	AI usage training or business strategy	Entrepreneurs or teams
Agency Owner	AI-powered copy, branding, or SEO packages	Business clients
Educator	AI course or mini-class	Students via Teachable or Skillshare

You don't need to be a programmer. You need **a marketable skill + AI + a platform.**

Tools to Boost Your Work with LLMs

- **ChatGPT** (Pro for GPT-4 recommended)
- **Claude** (great for long documents and summaries)
- **Writesonic or Jasper** (for faster marketing copy)
- **Notion AI** (for planning and content structure)
- **PromptBase** (to find and sell effective prompts)

These tools help you **produce faster and serve better**, so you can take on more work—or build scalable products.

Tips for Standing Out

1. **Edit and personalize**
   Don't just copy-paste from ChatGPT. Polish it. Humanize it. Add your voice.
2. **Niche down**
   Instead of being a general writer, be:

- "The ChatGPT expert for real estate emails"
- "An AI-powered ghostwriter for coaches"
- "A digital product creator for wellness businesses"

1. **Show your work**
   Create a portfolio. Record a demo. Use social proof. Most clients won't care how the work is made—they just want results.
2. **Sell the outcome, not the tool**
   Nobody pays you for "using ChatGPT." They pay for:

- More traffic
- More leads
- Less work
- Faster results

Start Simple

Still unsure where to begin?

Start by:

- Writing a blog post for a friend using ChatGPT
- Selling a prompt bundle on Gumroad
- Creating a free AI-powered newsletter
- Posting daily tips about LLMs on social media

You'll learn faster by **doing**, not by waiting.

⬦ Reflection & Action: Chapter 6 – Making Money with ChatGPT and Other LLMs

Reflect:

1. Which monetization model feels most aligned with your current skills or interests: freelancing, digital products, coaching, or education?
2. What is one specific use case for ChatGPT that could directly save you time or generate income?
3. How can you add your personal touch or expertise to stand out from others using the same tools?

Journal Prompt:

"If I could create one income-generating service or product using ChatGPT this month, it would be..."

Take Action:

⬦ 1. Define Your First Offer

Choose one simple offer you could launch this week using ChatGPT:

- A 500-word blog post for businesses
- A "10 LinkedIn post ideas" prompt pack
- A one-page resume rewrite
- A mini ebook for a niche audience

◈ **2. Write and Polish with ChatGPT**

Use ChatGPT to generate the content—but **don't stop there**. Edit it. Add your voice. Format it. Make it shine.

◈ **3. Publish It**

Upload it to a platform (Gumroad, Etsy, LinkedIn, Fiverr—whatever fits). Don't overthink. Done is better than perfect.

◈ **Bonus:**

Post about what you made on social media. Share your process. You never know who's watching—or who might become your first customer.

Power Quote:

"Don't wait for opportunity. Create it."

— George Bernard Shaw

Chapter 7: AI Content Creation for Profit

The Digital Content Explosion

Content is the currency of the internet. Businesses need it. Influencers live on it. Brands grow through it. And now, with AI, creating content is faster and cheaper than ever before—**which means you can profit from it at scale.**

Whether it's writing, visuals, audio, or video, AI tools give you the power to **create more content in less time** and offer it as a service, product, or personal brand.

If you can generate value with words or visuals, **you can monetize that skill.**

Types of Content You Can Create with AI

1. Written Content

- Blog posts
- Social media captions
- Email newsletters
- Scripts for YouTube or podcasts
- Course modules and lesson plans

2. Visual Content

- Instagram graphics

- Pinterest pins
- T-shirt designs
- Ebook covers
- YouTube thumbnails

3. Video & Audio Content

- Voiceovers
- Explainer videos
- Animated shorts
- TikTok or Instagram reels
- Audiograms or podcast teasers

Monetization Methods

Content Type	Monetization Options
Blog Posts	Offer writing services, publish on Medium or your site with ads/affiliate links
Social Captions	Sell social media packages to businesses
Templates	Sell on Etsy, Gumroad, or your website
Designs	Print-on-demand (Redbubble, TeeSpring), or sell digital assets
Videos	Monetize via YouTube, course platforms, or freelance gigs
Voiceovers	Offer narration, ad voice, podcast intros

Powerful Tools to Use

For Writing:

- ChatGPT (GPT-4)
- Jasper AI
- Writesonic
- Notion AI

For Visuals:

- Canva (with Magic Write & Magic Design)
- Leonardo.Ai
- Midjourney

- Adobe Firefly

For Audio/Video:

- ElevenLabs (voice cloning)
- Pictory (text-to-video)
- Synthesia (AI avatars)
- Descript (audio editing & transcription)

How to Stand Out as an AI Creator

1. **Be original.**
   Don't just create AI content—curate, edit, and enhance it. Add your personality. Add a hook. Add context.
2. **Target a niche.**
   Instead of "motivational content," try "wellness reels for busy moms." Instead of "ebooks," create "nutrition guides for college students."
3. **Batch and schedule.**
   Use AI to create a month's worth of content in a single afternoon, then automate your posting.
4. **Offer packages.**
   Bundle your content into ready-to-buy offers:

- 30 social captions + 10 graphics
- 5 blog posts + keyword research
- 10 voiceovers for podcast intros

From Content Creator to Business Owner

The real money comes when you:

- **Package your content into products**
- **License your work to others**
- **Build a content-based brand that attracts sponsors, buyers, and opportunities**

This chapter isn't just about making content. It's about **turning content into cashflow.**

⟐ Reflection & Action: Chapter 7 – AI Content Creation for Profit

Reflect:

1. What kind of content do you enjoy consuming or creating the most—written, visual, or video/audio?
2. Can you identify a niche you're interested in that you could serve with AI-generated content?
3. What limiting belief might be stopping you from publishing your content publicly?

Journal Prompt:

"If I committed to publishing one piece of AI-generated content every day for 30 days, I believe it would help me..."

Take Action:

⟐ 1. Choose Your Format

Decide what kind of content you want to create first:

- A blog post
- An Instagram carousel
- A T-shirt or merch design
- A TikTok or YouTube Short
- A digital planner, guide, or ebook

◈ 2. Use AI to Create It

Pick a tool based on your format:

- **Writing** → ChatGPT, Jasper
- **Design** → Canva, Leonardo.Ai
- **Video** → Pictory, Synthesia
- **Audio** → ElevenLabs, Descript

◈ 3. Publish and Share

Post your content on one platform (Medium, TikTok, Etsy, YouTube, LinkedIn—anywhere).

Don't worry about perfection. Focus on **shipping**.

◈ Bonus:

Add a call to action:

- "Want more like this?"
- "DM me to collaborate."
- "Available now on my Gumroad."

Power Quote:
"Content is fire; social media is gasoline."
— Jay Baer

Chapter 8: Designing and Selling AI Art

Art Meets Algorithms

Not long ago, digital art required a deep knowledge of Photoshop or years of drawing skill. Today, you can create stunning, sellable artwork in minutes using AI tools—no formal art training required.

This has opened the door for **a new kind of creative entrepreneur**: the AI artist.

Whether you want to sell prints, design merch, create digital downloads, or license your work—AI art can be a powerful (and profitable) creative hustle.

What Is AI Art?

AI-generated art uses machine learning models—like **Midjourney**, **Leonardo.Ai**, or **DALL·E**—to create visuals based on written prompts.

You simply describe what you want to see, and the AI creates it.

Examples:

- "A neon tiger walking through Tokyo in the rain"
- "Minimalist line art of a Black woman meditating"
- "Fantasy landscape with crystal mountains and floating islands"

Each prompt produces unique, high-quality imagery in seconds.

Popular Products You Can Create

Product Type	Where to Sell It
Printable wall art	Etsy, Gumroad, Redbubble
T-shirt & hoodie designs	Printful, TeeSpring, Merch by Amazon
Stickers & phone cases	Society6, Zazzle
Coloring books	Amazon KDP
AI art packs / bundles	Creative Market, Ko-fi
NFT collections	OpenSea, Foundation

The possibilities are endless—and most require **no upfront inventory**.

Tools to Use

- **Midjourney** – Powerful, stylized visuals; ideal for fantasy, portrait, and abstract art
- **Leonardo.Ai** – Great for product designs and UI elements
- **DALL·E** – Clean, surreal, and easy to use
- **Canva + AI** – Design templates, combine AI art with text for social media graphics
- **Creative Fabrica Spark** – Designed for print-on-demand creators

How to Stand Out as an AI Artist

1. Learn the art of prompting

Great AI art comes from great prompts. Master how to describe your desired styles, colors, lighting, compositions, and themes.

2. Focus on a niche or aesthetic

Instead of being all over the place, brand yourself around one visual identity:

- Afro-futurist posters
- Retro sci-fi book covers
- Dreamy spiritual mandalas
- Dark academia fashion designs

3. Combine human touch + AI

Enhance your AI art with Photoshop, Canva, or Procreate. Add filters, text overlays, or texture. Make it yours.

4. Build a storefront

Set up shop on platforms like Etsy or Redbubble, or create your own website with Shopify or Gumroad. Treat your AI art like a **business**, not just a hobby.

Legal & Ethical Considerations

- **Commercial rights:** Always check the terms of use for the tool you're using. Many platforms (like Midjourney or Leonardo) allow commercial use with paid plans.
- **Originality:** Don't copy artists or claim human authorship for AI-generated work. Be transparent about your process.

- **Trademark awareness:** Avoid using copyrighted characters, logos, or celebrity likenesses in your work.

You Don't Need to Be an Artist to Sell Art

You just need:

- A vision
- A prompt
- A platform
- A willingness to learn and create consistently

AI tools don't replace creativity—they **amplify it**.

⟐ Reflection & Action: Chapter 8 – Designing and Selling AI Art

Reflect:

1. What type of AI-generated art would you be most excited to create—wall art, merch, book covers, or something else?
2. Which platform (Etsy, Redbubble, Gumroad, etc.) feels like the right fit for your style or goals?
3. What would your art niche or visual identity be if you focused on one aesthetic?

Journal Prompt:

_"If I launched an AI art store tomorrow, I'd call it ________ and it would focus on _______."

Take Action:

◈ 1. Choose Your AI Art Tool

Pick one platform to explore:

- **Midjourney** for stylized creative art
- **Leonardo.Ai** for product design and fantasy visuals
- **DALL·E** for simple, surreal, or commercial graphics

◈ 2. Generate 3 Test Images

Use descriptive prompts to create three images that could be used as:

- A poster
- A T-shirt design
- A digital wallpaper

◈ 3. Publish a Sample

Upload your best piece to:

- Etsy (as a digital download)
- Redbubble (as merch)
- Instagram or Pinterest (to build an audience)

Include a title, description, and story behind the piece.

◈ Bonus:

Start a folder or workspace for "AI Art Business Ideas." Every time inspiration hits, jot it down.

Power Quote:

"Creativity is seeing what everyone else has seen, and thinking what no one else has thought."

— Albert Einstein

Chapter 9: Building an AI-Powered Newsletter

Email Isn't Dead—It's Dominating

With all the buzz around social media, you might think email is old news. But here's the truth:

Email is still one of the highest-converting, most personal, and most profitable tools online.

And thanks to AI, you no longer need to be a professional writer or marketing guru to start a high-value newsletter that earns money.

This chapter will show you how to use AI to **plan, write, grow, and monetize** your own niche email newsletter—from scratch.

Why Start a Newsletter?

- **You own your audience.** No algorithms. No shadowbans.
- **Email has high engagement.** People check it every day.
- **You can build trust over time.** And trust = sales.
- **It's a low-cost business.** You can start for free.
- **Monetization is simple.** Ads, affiliate links, products, or paid subscriptions.

And with AI, you can do in **30 minutes** what used to take 3 hours.

Types of AI-Powered Newsletters

Newsletter Niche	Possible Focus
Tech & AI	Weekly AI tool reviews, news summaries, trends
Finance & Crypto	Market recaps, stock picks, blockchain updates
Lifestyle & Wellness	Healthy habits, affirmations, productivity tips
Writing & Creativity	Prompts, tutorials, content tips
Business & Marketing	Growth hacks, tools, automation strategies
Pop Culture	TV/film breakdowns, trending stories, hot takes

How AI Can Help You Build It

Planning & Research

- Use **ChatGPT** or **Claude** to generate content calendars, brainstorm angles, and identify audience pain points.

Writing & Editing

- Draft newsletters in seconds with ChatGPT or Jasper.
- Use **Grammarly** or **Notion AI** for tone, structure, and clarity.

Design

- Use **Canva** to design headers, templates, and social graphics to promote the newsletter.

Automation & Growth

• Use tools like **Beehiiv**, **ConvertKit**, or **Substack** to automate delivery and subscriber management.

• Use **Zapier** to connect your sign-up forms to your email list, CRM, or content workflows.

How to Monetize Your Newsletter

1. **Affiliate links**
   Promote tools, books, or products related to your topic—and earn a commission per click or sale.
2. **Sponsored posts**
   Once you grow your subscriber list, brands will pay to reach your audience.
3. **Digital product sales**
   Link to your ebooks, templates, or courses inside your email.
4. **Paid subscriptions**
   Charge a monthly fee for exclusive content, coaching, or reports.
5. **Upsell services**
   Use your newsletter to funnel leads into higher-priced offers like consulting or coaching.

Getting Started in 3 Simple Steps

1. **Pick a niche you can stick with.**
   You don't need to be an expert—you just need to **be consistent and curious.**
2. **Commit to one email per week.**

Start small. Use AI to help. Build trust.

3. **Choose a free platform and start collecting emails.**
   Try **Beehiiv**, **Substack**, or **ConvertKit**. You don't need a website—just a good idea and a signup form.

You don't need a huge list to start making money. You need a clear focus, strong content, and one person who's willing to pay attention. Then two. Then ten. Then hundreds.

◈ Reflection & Action: Chapter 9 – Building an AI-Powered Newsletter

Reflect:

1. What topics or passions could you talk or write about every week without getting bored?
2. Who is one person—real or imagined—that would benefit from the content you could share in a newsletter?
3. What's held you back from starting a newsletter in the past—and how can AI help you overcome that?

Journal Prompt:
_"If I started an email newsletter tomorrow, it would be called ________ and help people ______."

Take Action:
◈ 1. Define Your Newsletter Idea
Answer these three questions:

- What's the topic?
- Who is it for?

- What's the promise/value of subscribing?

◈ 2. Create Your First Draft with ChatGPT

Prompt:

"Write a 300-word newsletter about [topic] that includes a personal intro, 2 key takeaways, and a call to action."

Polish it. Personalize it. Make it your voice.

◈ 3. Launch Your Signup Page

Choose a platform:

- **Beginner-friendly:**Substack.com[1]
- **Growth-focused:**Beehiiv.com[2]
- **Feature-rich:**ConvertKit.com[3]

Add your logo, a short pitch, and a signup button. Share it on social media—even if just once.

◈ Bonus:

Invite 5 friends to subscribe and give feedback. Your audience starts with **one relationship at a time.**

Power Quote:

"Build a list. Build a business. Build a life."

— David Moore

---

1. https://www.substack.com
2. https://www.beehiiv.com
3. https://www.convertkit.com

Chapter 10: Voiceovers and Audiobooks Using AI Tools

Speak Up—Without Saying a Word

Voice is one of the most intimate, engaging formats available today. It's used in everything from podcasts and YouTube videos to explainer ads, audiobooks, and even TikTok narration. And with AI voice tools, you no longer need a microphone—or even your own voice—to get started.

This chapter is all about **turning spoken content into income**, using the power of synthetic voice generators.

What You Can Create with AI Voice Tools

Content Type	Where to Sell or Use It
Audiobooks	Amazon ACX, Payhip, Spotify
Podcast voiceovers	Your own show or freelance gigs
Ad narration	Freelance marketplaces or Fiverr
YouTube/Shorts narration	Monetize your own channels or offer as a service
Guided meditations	Insight Timer, Gumroad, personal brand
Language tutorials	Sell as digital products or offer subscription content
TikTok or Reels voiceovers	Build a following or produce for influencers

AI makes these opportunities **low-cost and low-barrier**—and the quality is more realistic than ever.

Recommended AI Voice Tools

- **ElevenLabs** – Industry-leading voice realism; clone your own voice or choose from dozens of natural styles
- **Play.ht** – Great for converting long-form text to audio
- **Lovo.ai** – Excellent for audiobooks, podcasts, and training videos
- **Descript** – Includes Overdub voice cloning + full podcast editing
- **Murf.ai** – Business-grade voiceovers for presentations and corporate work
- **Synthesia.io** – Combine AI voice with talking avatars for videos

Real Monetization Paths

1. Freelance Voice Services

Offer fast, professional AI voiceovers to:

- Authors needing audiobooks
- Coaches needing meditations
- YouTubers who don't want to speak
- Marketers who need explainer videos
- App developers needing instructions

List your service on Fiverr, Upwork, or Voice123.

2. Create Your Own Audio Products

Use AI voice to:

- Narrate your ebooks
- Create a short course or tutorial
- Launch a guided audio journal
- Make a daily affirmation podcast

You don't need a fancy studio—just an idea and an AI voice.

3. Enhance Your Content with Voice

Add AI narration to your:

- Instagram Reels
- TikToks
- Twitter threads
- LinkedIn content

This adds value and increases accessibility for your audience.

How to Make Your Voiceovers Stand Out

- **Write engaging scripts.** Use ChatGPT to create snappy, emotionally resonant scripts with hooks and clear calls to action.
- **Edit and mix.** Use Descript, GarageBand, or Audacity to adjust pacing, add music, and refine the sound.

- **Match tone to audience.** Choose a voice style that fits the niche—soothing for meditation, upbeat for fitness, formal for business.

Legal and Ethical Tips

- Always check the licensing and commercial usage rights for any AI tool you use.
- Be transparent if you're selling audio products made with synthetic voices.
- Avoid using AI to imitate or clone celebrities or public figures without consent.
- For audiobook platforms like **ACX**, verify if AI narration is allowed. (Some now support it; others require human narration.)

You don't need a radio voice. You don't need a studio.

All you need is an idea, a script, and a tool that speaks for you.

◈ Reflection & Action: Chapter 10 – Voiceovers and Audiobooks Using AI Tools

Reflect:

1. What kind of audio content excites you most—meditations, audiobooks, YouTube narration, or something else?
2. Could you see yourself using AI voice tools to create passive income products, freelance services, or personal content?

3. What voice tone or style (calm, bold, quirky, professional) best fits your ideal audience?

Journal Prompt:

"If my voice could teach, inspire, or entertain others—even if it's AI-generated—it would be through..."

Take Action:

◈ 1. Pick a Tool to Explore

Choose an AI voice platform to try:

- **ElevenLabs** – For narration and audiobook realism
- **Lovo.ai** – For explainer videos or business voiceovers
- **Murf.ai** – For professional training or corporate content
- **Descript** – For editing and voice cloning

◈ 2. Create a Sample Voiceover

Use ChatGPT to write a short 30–60 second script based on a topic you love or want to monetize. Then convert it to voice using your selected tool.

◈ 3. Share It or Package It

Upload the sample to:

- Social media (Instagram, YouTube, TikTok)
- Fiverr or Upwork portfolio
- Your website or sales page (for audio products)

◈ Bonus:

Create an "Audio Product Ideas" note and list 3 monetizable audio ideas:

- Guided journaling series
- Audiobook version of your ebook
- Voiceover package for online creators

Power Quote:
"The human voice is the most powerful sound on the planet. With AI, it's now the most scalable."
— David Moore

Chapter 11: AI-Powered Freelance Services

Freelancing Just Got a Major Upgrade

In the old days, freelancers had to choose between speed and quality. Today, with AI at your side, you can offer both—and at scale. Whether you're a writer, designer, strategist, or total beginner, AI can help you **deliver faster, charge more, and serve more clients.**

Freelancers who know how to use AI tools aren't just more efficient—they're more profitable.

Let's break down how to turn your AI skills into freelance income streams.

Why Freelancing with AI Works

- **Higher output with less burnout**
- **More competitive pricing** with faster turnaround
- **Smaller learning curve** for new skills
- **Room to niche down** and scale up

You're not just selling services. You're selling **speed, consistency, and value**—all powered by AI.

In-Demand Freelance Services You Can Offer with AI

Service	AI Tools to Use	Where to Offer It
Blog & web writing	ChatGPT, Jasper	Fiverr, Upwork, LinkedIn
SEO research & content	Surfer SEO, Writesonic	SEO agencies, freelancers
Social media posts	Canva, Copy.ai	Instagram marketers, coaches
Email marketing	Mailchimp + ChatGPT	Shopify brands, authors
Design & branding	Midjourney, Leonardo.Ai	Etsy, Behance, 99Designs
Scriptwriting	ChatGPT, Notion AI	YouTubers, agencies
Resume writing	Rezi, ChatGPT	LinkedIn, career coaches
Video editing + scripts	Pictory, Descript	TikTokers, course creators

Step-by-Step: Launch Your AI-Powered Freelance Hustle

Step 1: Choose a service you can deliver with AI help

Pick something that interests you AND solves a problem. Even if you're not an expert, AI can level the playing field.

Step 2: Create a polished offer

Write a service description that highlights:

- What you do
- How fast you deliver
- What tools you use

- What results clients can expect

Step 3: Build a simple portfolio
Use AI to create a few "mock" samples. For example:

- 3 blog post intros
- 5 Instagram captions
- 1 branding concept
- 1 newsletter issue

Step 4: Set up shop
Post your offer on:

- **Freelance platforms:** Fiverr, Upwork, Freelancer
- **Business groups:** Facebook groups, Reddit, Discord
- **Social platforms:** LinkedIn, Twitter, TikTok

And be direct: "I help [target audience] get [result] using AI-enhanced [your service]."

Step 5: Start pitching
Reach out to 5–10 people each week. Keep it short, specific, and client-focused.

Pro Tips for AI Freelancers

- **Don't sell the tool—sell the result.** Clients don't care if you use AI. They care if you save them time, make them money, or get them noticed.

- **Personalize the work.** AI gets you 80% of the way. That final 20%—your taste, your edits, your creativity—is where your value shines.

- **Create packages.** Instead of charging per piece, offer bundled deals:

  - "5 blog posts for $200"

  - "30 captions for $150"

  - "Full branding kit for $300"

- **Keep learning.** The tools will evolve. Stay curious, test new features, and continue improving your workflow.

What If You Don't Have Clients Yet?

Start small. Offer free work to 1–2 local businesses in exchange for a testimonial. Or create fake sample projects to demonstrate your skill.

What matters is that you start. Freelance income isn't reserved for pros—it's earned through practice and persistence.

◈ Reflection & Action: Chapter 11 – AI-Powered Freelance Services

Reflect:

1. Which freelance service listed in this chapter feels like the best fit for your skills and interests?
2. How could you use AI to improve your delivery speed, client results, or offer value others can't?

3. What's one fear or hesitation you have about freelancing—and what's one way to test your idea with minimal risk?

Journal Prompt:
_"If I offered one AI-powered freelance service this month, it would be _______ for ______."

Take Action:
◈ 1. Choose Your Starter Service
Pick **one** of the following (or your own) to focus on this week:

- Write 3 blog posts
- Create a batch of Instagram captions
- Design a logo + brand board using Midjourney and Canva
- Generate a newsletter and offer it to a creator or coach

◈ 2. Use AI to Build Your Portfolio
Even if you don't have clients yet, create:

- 1–3 sample pieces
- A brief write-up explaining what you did and why
- A one-page PDF or link to share your work

◈ 3. Post Your Offer
Choose **one platform** to launch:

- Fiverr, Upwork, Contra, PeoplePerHour

- LinkedIn (make a post and update your headline)
- Twitter or Reddit (freelance or creator communities)

◈ **Bonus:**

Send **3 cold messages** today. Keep it simple:

"Hi [Name], I help [type of business] create [type of content] using AI—faster and more affordably than traditional agencies. Can I show you a free sample?"

Power Quote:

"Don't wait until you're ready. The market rewards action, not perfection."

— David Moore

Chapter 12: AI for Social Media Management

The Attention Economy Is Automated

In today's digital world, attention is currency—and **social media is the bank.** But managing content, engagement, and strategy across multiple platforms is time-consuming and overwhelming.

That's why businesses, influencers, and creators are **outsourcing**. And if you know how to use AI to streamline the process, you can turn social media management into a **steady income stream.**

This chapter shows you how to use AI tools to plan, create, schedule, and optimize social content—without burning out or getting lost in the algorithm.

Why AI Social Media Management Works

- **Content is king**—and brands need a LOT of it
- **AI writes, designs, and repurposes** content fast
- **Scheduling and analytics tools automate the rest**
- **Most small businesses and creators don't have time** to do it all themselves

Your job? **Use AI to fill that gap—and get paid for it.**

AI Tools That Supercharge Social Media Work

Writing & Captioning:

- **ChatGPT** – For ideas, captions, hooks, and hashtags
- **Jasper AI** – For branded, tone-specific posts
- **Copy.ai** – Fast, editable content for multiple platforms

Design & Visuals:

- **Canva** – Pre-made templates + Magic Design AI
- **Leonardo.Ai** – Custom illustrations or digital assets
- **Midjourney** – Eye-catching art for viral posts

Scheduling & Optimization:

- **Metricool** – All-in-one content planner with analytics
- **Buffer** or **Later** – Plan and schedule posts across platforms
- **ChatGPT + Zapier** – Auto-generate & post content via workflows

Analytics & Growth:

- **Predis.ai** – Analyzes your content and suggests high-performers
- **Notion AI** – Track growth, trends, and engagement patterns

Monetizable Services You Can Offer

Service	What You Provide	Monthly Rate Range
Content creation	Posts, captions, graphics	$300–$1,000
Full social media management	Strategy, scheduling, analytics	$750–$2,500
AI branding kits	Templates, bios, hashtags	$150–$600
Reels/TikTok scripting	Viral video scripts with voiceover prompts	$100–$500
Repurposing content	Turning blogs/podcasts into social clips	$200–$800

Many freelancers use AI to manage **5–10 clients per month** and scale from there.

Getting Started as an AI Social Media Manager

1. Choose a niche or platform.

- Instagram for wellness brands
- LinkedIn for coaches
- TikTok for small retailers

Start focused so you can deliver better results and position yourself as a specialist.

2. Create a sample week of content.
Use ChatGPT + Canva to design:

- 3–5 branded posts

- Hashtags and hooks
- Scheduling calendar

3. Set up your offer.
Define your packages:

- Content only?
- Content + posting?
- Full management + reporting?

4. Reach out.
DM local business owners, influencers, or solopreneurs. Offer to manage their content for a week at a discount or for a testimonial.

Pro Tips

- **Don't overpromise.** AI can do a lot, but strategy still matters. Focus on clear, realistic deliverables.
- **Automate wisely.** Use automation to reduce workload, not eliminate human oversight.
- **Track results.** Use metrics like reach, engagement, saves, and click-through rates to prove value.

If you can help people show up online consistently and confidently—you're not just a social media manager. You're a **growth partner.**

And thanks to AI, you can do it **faster and smarter than ever.**

◈ Reflection & Action: Chapter 12 – AI for Social Media Management

Reflect:

1. Which social media platform do you enjoy the most—or understand best?
2. Could you see yourself helping businesses or creators improve their online presence using AI tools?
3. What's one fear or obstacle that's stopped you from offering social media services before?

Journal Prompt:

_"If I became a go-to AI-powered social media expert for one niche, it would be ________ because _______."

Take Action:

◈ 1. Pick Your Platform + Niche

Choose a combination that feels natural and aligned with your strengths. Example:

- Instagram + health coaches
- TikTok + handmade shops
- LinkedIn + solopreneurs

◈ 2. Build a 3-Day Content Sample

Use:

- **ChatGPT** to write captions and hashtags
- **Canva** to create graphics
- **Metricool or Buffer** to schedule (even as a demo)

◈ **3. Offer a Free Trial to 1–2 Clients**

Reach out via DM or email. Say:

"Hey! I'm testing a new AI-powered content system for [niche]. I'd love to create 3–5 posts for you to test—free, no strings. If you love it, we can talk about monthly options."

◈ **Bonus:**

Track post performance and turn it into a case study you can share.

Power Quote:

"In the age of content overload, consistency wins—and AI makes it effortless."

— David Moore

Chapter 13: Virtual Assistance with AI Tools

The Rise of the Super-VA

Virtual assistants (VAs) have become essential to entrepreneurs, coaches, and small businesses. But today's most in-demand VAs aren't just task-doers—they're **problem-solvers armed with AI tools.**

If you can combine basic admin skills with AI-powered productivity, you can offer **high-value services** without burning yourself out—and earn more in less time.

This chapter is all about using AI to become a **Super-VA**—faster, smarter, and ready to scale.

What a Modern AI-Enhanced VA Can Do

Service Area	How AI Helps You
Email Management	Use ChatGPT to write, sort, and respond to emails faster
Calendar & Scheduling	Use AI tools to automate bookings, reminders, and follow-ups
Content Repurposing	Convert blogs into reels, emails, and quotes using AI
Research	Use Claude or ChatGPT for market summaries, competitor research
Admin Support	Auto-generate docs, proposals, SOPs, and meeting notes
Social Media	Create posts, captions, and basic designs with AI
Customer Service	Write canned replies, FAQs, and scripts using ChatGPT
Project Management	Use Notion AI or Trello AI plugins for smart planning

With the right tools, you can serve **more clients** with **less manual work**—and charge accordingly.

Top AI Tools for Virtual Assistants

- **ChatGPT** – For emails, summaries, replies, drafts, SOPs
- **Notion AI** – For task lists, meeting notes, workflows
- **Calendly + Zapier** – For smart scheduling and automation
- **Pictory or Descript** – For video snippets or transcription

- **Trello + Butler AI** – For managing team workflows
- **Canva** – For light design work (with templates and AI-powered features)

Real Client Needs You Can Fulfill

Client Type	What They Need
Coaches	Email funnels, calendar management, content snippets
E-commerce stores	Order replies, product listings, newsletters
Course creators	Lesson formatting, content repurposing, community moderation
Solopreneurs	Inbox zero, scheduling, system building
Podcasters	Show notes, repurposed clips, guest research

How to Launch Your AI-Powered VA Service

Step 1: Define your specialty.

Don't be a "do-it-all VA." Pick 2–3 high-impact services to focus on.

Example: "I'm a virtual assistant who helps coaches automate their content and inbox."

Step 2: Create a starter package.

Bundle your services into a monthly plan:

- 10 emails/week + 2 content repurposes + calendar updates = $500/month

- Full VA support with AI-enhanced workflows = $750–$1,200/month

Step 3: Test your tools.

Use free trials of Notion AI, Zapier, or Descript. Build a "client folder" and simulate managing a business for practice.

Step 4: Start pitching.

Reach out to people in online communities—coaches, course creators, small business groups—and offer a 7-day trial or free audit of their digital workflows.

The Key: Sell Your Value, Not the Tech

Most clients don't care about the AI tools—they care about:

- Having more free time
- Getting consistent communication
- Feeling like someone has their back

Use AI to deliver **that level of support—faster, smoother, and smarter.**

◈ Reflection & Action: Chapter 13 – Virtual Assistance with AI Tools

Reflect:

1. What types of tasks do you naturally enjoy helping others with—organizing, writing, researching, designing, etc.?
2. Which industries or client types (coaches, podcasters, creators, etc.) would you be excited to support?

3. How could using AI help you serve more clients without feeling overwhelmed?

Journal Prompt:

_"If I built a VA business using AI, I would focus on helping _______ with ______."

Take Action:

◈ 1. Identify Your "Power Services"

Choose 2–3 high-value VA tasks that you can confidently offer, powered by AI.

Examples:

- Calendar & inbox management
- Social post repurposing
- Meeting notes + project updates
- Customer service replies

◈ 2. Build a Sample Workflow

Create a "Client Task Simulation" using:

- **ChatGPT** to draft emails or summarize meeting notes
- **Notion AI** to organize a project board
- **Canva** to design a weekly recap template

◈ 3. Create a Starter Offer

Package your services into a beginner-friendly offer, such as:

- "2 weeks of inbox, calendar, and content support for $99"

- "Monthly automation + admin package for busy solopreneurs"

Then share it on LinkedIn, Instagram, or in small business communities.

◈ **Bonus:**

Write a short case study (real or mock) showing how AI helped you complete 3 hours of admin work in just 45 minutes.

Power Quote:

"Smart people delegate. Smarter people automate first, then delegate better."

— David Moore

Chapter 14: Resume and Cover Letter Services with AI

From Job Hunt Stress to Job Land Success

Resumes and cover letters are often a job seeker's biggest headache—and your biggest opportunity.

Most people:

- Hate writing about themselves
- Don't know what hiring managers want
- Submit bland, generic applications that get ignored

With AI, you can step in and **transform job searches into job offers**—by offering fast, personalized, professional resume services powered by tools like ChatGPT.

Why This Niche Works

- The job market is competitive—everyone wants an edge
- Most people don't know how to "sell themselves"
- AI can draft strong resumes fast, but people still want a human touch
- You can charge \$50–\$500 per client for short, high-impact projects

This is a perfect service for career coaches, freelance writers, or anyone who wants to help people **get hired faster.**

What You Can Offer

Service	Deliverables
Resume revamp	Updated format, optimized content, targeted keywords
Cover letter writing	Customized letters for specific roles
LinkedIn profile upgrade	Bio rewrite, headline, featured content
Job search templates	Thank-you emails, follow-up scripts, networking intros
Full application bundle	Resume + cover + LinkedIn + interview prep scripts

You can create this all in **less than 2 hours** per client using AI.

Recommended Tools

- **ChatGPT** – Use prompts to draft resumes, cover letters, and bios
- **Resumake.io** – Free resume builder with clean templates
- **Rezi.ai** – AI resume optimization for ATS (Applicant Tracking Systems)
- **Jobscan** – Match resumes to job descriptions for keyword alignment
- **Canva** – Clean, modern visual resumes and portfolio designs
- **Grammarly** – Final polish for clarity, tone, and grammar

How to Build a Resume Service from Scratch

Step 1: Learn the Basics

Study a few good resume examples. Watch YouTube videos on what makes resumes stand out. Understand ATS (resume screening software).

Step 2: Build a Sample Portfolio

Use ChatGPT to:

- Rewrite your own resume
- Create 2–3 fictional client resumes
- Draft sample cover letters for mock job listings

Step 3: Create Simple Packages

Offer clear, entry-level bundles like:

- Resume only: $99
- Resume + cover letter: $149
- Resume + LinkedIn + coaching: $299+

Step 4: Find Clients

Post in:

- Facebook job search and career groups
- Reddit communities like r/resumes or r/jobs
- Local networking groups
- Fiverr, Upwork, or LinkedIn Services Marketplace

Offer a "first client" discount or a free mini-review to build testimonials.

Pro Tips

- **Don't sound robotic.** Use AI for structure, then add a personal, human polish.
- **Always tailor to the job posting.** Use ChatGPT to compare the job ad to the resume—then optimize.
- **Use metrics.** Add quantifiable achievements whenever possible.
- **Track your results.** If a client gets interviews or lands a job, that becomes powerful marketing.

Helping someone land their dream job doesn't just make you money—it makes an impact.

With AI on your side, you can offer high-quality, fast-turnaround services that people actually need—and are happy to pay for.

◈ Reflection & Action: Chapter 14 – Resume and Cover Letter Services with AI

Reflect:

1. Have you ever struggled with writing your own resume or cover letter? What made it difficult?
2. Can you think of someone in your network who might benefit from a professionally written resume?

3. What's one way you could use AI to make the job application process easier or more effective for others?

Journal Prompt:
_"If I could help people get hired faster using AI, I'd focus on _______ job seekers and help them with ______."

Take Action:
◈ **1. Build a Sample Resume Bundle**
Use ChatGPT to create a mock set for a fictional job seeker:

- 1-page resume for a marketing coordinator
- Cover letter tailored to a real job posting
- LinkedIn profile headline + summary
- Thank-you email after the interview

◈ **2. Create a "Before and After" Portfolio**
Design a simple document that shows:

- Original resume (cluttered, generic)
- AI-enhanced version (clean, targeted, results-based)

Use Canva or Google Docs for a clean layout.

◈ **3. Offer a Free Resume Review**
Post in a career-focused Facebook group, subreddit, or LinkedIn update offering:

"Free resume audit for 3 job seekers today—get AI-powered insights and fast upgrades to stand out and land more interviews."

◈ **Bonus:**

Keep track of client results. When they get interviews or jobs, ask for testimonials or referrals.

Power Quote:

"A strong resume opens doors. A smart resume gets you through them faster."

— David Moore

Chapter 15: AI Consulting for Small Businesses

The Advisors of the New Economy

Most small business owners have **heard** of AI—but very few understand how to actually **use it**. They're overwhelmed by tools, buzzwords, and uncertainty. That's where **you** come in.

AI consultants don't have to be engineers or data scientists. Many of the most successful ones are freelancers, marketers, or productivity pros who simply **know how to match the right tool to the right business problem.**

If you can help businesses save time, increase revenue, or improve customer experience with AI—you can build a **high-ticket consulting offer.**

What Small Businesses Want from AI

Business Need	AI Solution
Save time on tasks	ChatGPT automation, Zapier workflows
Improve content output	Blog & social media generation
Boost customer service	Chatbots, FAQ builders, auto-responders
Personalize marketing	AI email tools, segmentation, lead scoring
Organize workflows	Notion AI, Airtable, project automation
Train staff	SOPs, onboarding videos using AI
Cut costs	Replace repetitive tasks with AI tools

Most business owners want results, **not tech talk**—which makes your ability to simplify and implement incredibly valuable.

How to Position Yourself as an AI Consultant

1. Choose a niche or type of business.

Examples:

- Local service providers (salons, gyms, clinics)
- E-commerce shops
- Coaches and course creators
- Real estate agencies
- Nonprofits or solopreneurs

2. Learn 5–10 AI tools deeply.

You don't need to know everything—just enough to recommend, demonstrate, and implement.

Key tools:

- ChatGPT
- Canva (for content)
- Zapier (for automations)
- Pictory or Synthesia (for training videos)
- Tidio or ManyChat (for chatbots)
- Notion AI or Trello (for internal workflows)

3. Create a signature service.

Example:

"AI Efficiency Audit for Small Businesses: Cut 10 hours/week using smart tools you already have access to."

Or:

"3-Week AI Accelerator: Turn your content, email, and customer support into automated systems."

Example Consulting Packages

Package	Includes	Price Range
AI Audit	1-hour consult + summary PDF	$150–$300
Implementation	Set up tools, automations, content systems	$500–$1,500
Training	AI playbooks, tutorials, staff onboarding	$1,000–$3,000
Retainer	Ongoing AI support and upgrades	$500+/month

You can deliver these virtually, making it scalable and flexible.

Where to Find Clients

- Local business groups (Facebook, Chamber of Commerce, Meetup)
- LinkedIn (especially industry-specific hashtags or groups)
- Cold email outreach to small biz websites
- Fiverr & Upwork under "business automation" or "productivity"
- Partner with agencies or VA firms who don't offer AI yet

Your Edge: Translating Complexity into Clarity

You're not just an AI tool expert. You're a **translator**—helping overwhelmed entrepreneurs understand how AI fits their business, without jargon.

When you can connect AI to **real-world outcomes** (saving time, getting leads, improving service), you become **indispensable.**

◈ Reflection & Action: Chapter 15 – AI Consulting for Small Businesses

Reflect:

1. What type of small business or entrepreneur would you love to help streamline their workflow or grow their brand?
2. Which AI tools do you already use well enough to teach or set up for someone else?
3. How confident are you in showing others how to simplify, automate, or delegate using AI—and where might you need to learn more?

Journal Prompt:

_"If I were hired to help a small business use AI, the first 3 things I'd optimize would be ______, ______, and _____."

Take Action:

◈ 1. Create a 1-Page AI Audit Template

Make a simple Google Doc with:

- A short questionnaire ("What's your biggest time-waster?")

- Tool suggestions for content, support, scheduling, or marketing

- A section for top 3 quick wins using AI

◈ 2. Choose 1 Niche + 3 Tools to Master
Example:

- Niche: Coaches

- Tools: ChatGPT (content), Calendly (scheduling), Notion AI (project planning)

◈ 3. Reach Out and Offer a Free Mini-Audit
Send messages or emails like:

"Hey [Name], I help [niche] save 5–10 hours a week using AI tools you probably already have access to. Want a free audit of where automation could boost your biz?"

◈ Bonus:

Turn your best audit into a before/after case study you can send in future pitches or feature on your site.

Power Quote:

"Small businesses don't need more tools. They need someone who can show them how to use the right ones the right way."

— David Moore

Chapter 16: Starting an AI Copywriting Agency

Words Still Sell—Now They Scale

Copy is the lifeblood of online business. Every email, ad, product page, and social post needs writing that persuades, informs, or converts. The problem? Most business owners don't have the time or skill to write copy that works.

That's where you—and AI—step in.

An AI-powered copywriting agency uses tools like ChatGPT, Jasper, and Copy.ai to **deliver high-volume, high-quality content fast**. You don't need to be a master writer—you just need to know how to craft prompts, edit results, and deliver messaging that moves people to action.

Why AI Copywriting Is in High Demand

- Content demand is exploding: blogs, email, social, ads, landing pages
- AI cuts writing time by 70–90%, increasing agency capacity
- Most small businesses can't afford full-time copywriters—but they'll pay a skilled AI-powered freelancer or agency
- Niches like coaches, e-commerce brands, and SaaS businesses need copy **every week**

This is your chance to turn simple AI outputs into **powerful sales assets**—and earn recurring revenue while you're at it.

Copywriting Services You Can Offer

Service	Typical Uses
Website copy	Home, About, Services, Landing Pages
Product descriptions	E-commerce listings, Amazon pages
Email marketing	Newsletters, automations, launches
Social media captions	Instagram, LinkedIn, Twitter, TikTok
Ad copy	Facebook, Google, YouTube, Pinterest
SEO blog posts	Long-form content, keyword optimized
Funnels	Sales pages, upsells, opt-in pages

Tools for Scaling Copy Fast

- **ChatGPT** – Great for first drafts, creative variations, tone shifts
- **Jasper** – Templates for ads, sales pages, email sequences
- **Copy.ai** – Good for idea generation, headline testing
- **Grammarly** – For clarity, tone, and grammar polish
- **Surfer SEO** – Optimizes long-form blog content for Google
- **Notion AI** – Organize SOPs, copy banks, client info

How to Launch Your AI Copywriting Agency

Step 1: Pick a Niche and Messaging Style

Do you want to write bold DTC e-com copy? Thoughtful B2B LinkedIn posts? Spiritual wellness emails? Choose a voice and stick with it.

Step 2: Build a Copy Portfolio

Use AI to:

- Create mock homepage copy for a pretend client
- Write 3 email promos for a fictional product
- Draft 2 social ad campaigns with different tones

Then edit, format, and publish it in a PDF, Notion page, or website.

Step 3: Craft Packages That Sell

Offer:

- 4 social posts/week = $150/month
- Monthly email sequence + 2 landing pages = $400
- Full launch copy bundle (emails, page, ads) = $1,000+

Step 4: Promote on Creator Platforms

- Twitter and LinkedIn (share before/after copy examples)
- Facebook Groups (coaches, creators, startups)
- Reddit (copywriting, entrepreneur, or freelance threads)
- Cold DM/email with portfolio link and a personalized pitch

How to Stand Out

- **Focus on results.** Show how your copy increases sales, clicks, or time-on-page.

- **Build systems.** Use AI to speed up drafts, templates, and processes.

- **Create retainer clients.** Don't just write once—offer monthly content plans.

- **Become a "voice match" expert.** Use ChatGPT to replicate tone, brand language, and customer emotions.

A copywriting agency powered by AI isn't about doing less—it's about **doing more for more people**, faster and better than ever before.

The businesses are out there. The demand is massive. The tools are waiting.

All you need is to start typing.

◈ Reflection & Action: Chapter 16 – Starting an AI Copywriting Agency

Reflect:

1. What kind of copy do you naturally gravitate toward—email, blogs, product descriptions, ads, etc.?
2. Which industries or niches could benefit most from fast, affordable AI-enhanced copywriting?
3. What strengths (tone, clarity, creativity, structure) could you

bring to polished AI-generated content?

Journal Prompt:

"If I built an AI copywriting agency tomorrow, I would help ______ by writing ______ that drives results."

Take Action:

◈ 1. Choose a Service Niche

Pick one high-value copy type to focus on for your first offer:

- Email copy
- Website or landing pages
- Blog posts
- Product descriptions
- Ads or captions

◈ 2. Create a Copywriting Sample Kit

Use ChatGPT or Jasper to draft 3–5 samples for fictional businesses.

Format them into a clean, branded PDF portfolio or Notion link.

◈ 3. Set Your Packages and Pricing

Example starter offers:

- 3 email promos for $99
- Weekly caption packs for $149/month
- Sales page + thank-you page for $249

◈ 4. Promote Your Offer

- DM a coach or creator and offer a free headline audit

- Post a side-by-side "bad vs. AI-enhanced" copy example on social media

- Send 5 cold emails with the subject line: "Need better copy, faster?"

◈ **Bonus:**
Use testimonials from your early clients to create a "copy that converts" case study you can repurpose everywhere.

Power Quote:
"Good copy sells. Great copy scales. AI lets you deliver both."
— David Moore

Chapter 17: Launching a Print-on-Demand Business with AI

Sell Merch Without Inventory or Risk

Print-on-demand (POD) lets you create and sell physical products—like T-shirts, hoodies, mugs, posters, journals, and more—**without holding any inventory.**

With AI on your side, you don't need to be a designer, trend forecaster, or branding expert. AI can generate your artwork, slogans, store descriptions, and even ads.

That means you can build a **passive income stream** selling physical goods online—while AI does most of the heavy lifting.

Why Print-on-Demand Works

- **No upfront cost for inventory or printing**
- **Zero shipping or fulfillment hassle**
- **Scalable product lines**—you can test and expand quickly
- **AI makes it easy to stand out** with unique, niche-targeted designs
- **High demand for gifts, lifestyle merch, niche apparel, and décor**

This is one of the **easiest, lowest-risk ways** to start an online store today.

AI Tools for Print-on-Demand Success

Design & Art Generation:

- **Midjourney** – Unique, stylized illustrations or themed artwork
- **Leonardo.Ai** – Print-ready mockups and designs
- **Canva AI** – Design templates, text overlays, product previews

Copy & Branding:

- **ChatGPT** – Write your store name, descriptions, SEO tags, slogans
- **Copy.ai** – Create product listings, social media ads, and more

Trend Research:

- **Pinterest + Etsy + Amazon** – See what's trending
- **Exploding Topics** – Track emerging micro-niches

Product Ideas to Start With

Product	AI Angle	Where to Sell
T-Shirts & Hoodies	Use AI to generate quotes, slogans, or art	Etsy, Redbubble, Merch by Amazon
Wall Art & Posters	Midjourney or DALL·E image designs	Etsy, Society6, Displate
Journals & Notebooks	AI-generated prompts or affirmations	Lulu xPress, Amazon KDP
Mugs & Drinkware	Funny sayings, custom patterns	TeeSpring, Printful
Phone Cases & Stickers	Niche slogans, minimalist art	Redbubble, Zazzle

How to Launch Your AI-Powered POD Brand

Step 1: Pick a niche

The riches are in the niches. Go specific.
Examples:

- Funny wellness affirmations
- Minimalist quotes for tech bros
- Witchy spiritual vibes
- Urban streetwear with AI art
- Motivational merch for side hustlers

Step 2: Design your first 3–5 products

Use AI tools to:

- Generate art (Midjourney, Leonardo.Ai)
- Write product names, descriptions, and keywords (ChatGPT)
- Add final touches in Canva

Step 3: Upload to a POD platform
Options:

- **Etsy + Printify or Printful**
- **Redbubble, Teespring, Zazzle**
- **Shopify + Printful (for more control)**

Step 4: Promote your brand

- Share behind-the-scenes of your AI art creation
- Use TikTok, Instagram, or Pinterest to post lifestyle mockups
- Run low-cost ads using your AI-generated copy and images

Bonus Monetization Tip

Package your best AI designs and sell them as **printable downloads** (for wall art, planners, coloring pages, etc.) on Etsy or Gumroad for **100% margin**—no printing or fulfillment required.

Print-on-demand is **a digital business dressed in physical clothes**—and AI is your secret fashion designer.

If you've ever wanted to sell products but hate the logistics, this is your chance to let creativity and automation build your storefront.

◈ Reflection & Action: Chapter 17 – Launching a Print-on-Demand Business with AI

Reflect:

1. What types of physical products (shirts, mugs, posters, etc.) do you personally love—or could see yourself designing?
2. Which niches or communities are you already part of or familiar with that could inspire product ideas?
3. What excites you most about creating a storefront using AI tools?

Journal Prompt:

_"If I launched a print-on-demand brand today, my niche would be ________ and my first product would be _______."

Take Action:

◈ 1. Pick a Niche + 3 Product Types

Examples:

- Niche: Gamers | Products: T-shirts, mousepads, stickers
- Niche: Motivational Moms | Products: Mugs, journals, wall prints
- Niche: Black culture + affirmations | Products: Hoodies, posters, tote bags

◈ 2. Design a 3-Product Starter Set
Use:

- **Midjourney or Leonardo.Ai** for artwork
- **ChatGPT** for slogans, product titles, and Etsy tags
- **Canva** to format mockups and product thumbnails

◈ 3. Choose a Platform and Upload Your Products

- Start with Etsy + Printify for ease
- Use Redbubble if you want to sell without customer service
- Launch on Shopify if you want a full brand experience

◈ Bonus:
Post your designs on social media with behind-the-scenes insights like:
"This design was created using AI + a quote that kept me going during hard times."

Power Quote:
"You don't need a warehouse to sell products anymore—just a great idea and the right tools."
— David Moore

Chapter 18: Building Chatbots for Businesses

24/7 Service, Zero Employees

In a world where speed and responsiveness are everything, chatbots are gold. They give customers instant answers, qualify leads, schedule appointments, and even close sales—all without human intervention.

Most small businesses want chatbots. Few know how to build them. That's your opportunity.

With the rise of **no-code AI chatbot tools**, you can start offering chatbot setup services for websites, ecommerce stores, coaches, consultants, and local businesses—**even if you're not a developer.**

What a Chatbot Can Do

Function	Use Case
Answer FAQs	Help desk, customer support, product info
Qualify leads	Collect emails, ask questions, score buyers
Schedule appointments	Connect to Calendly or booking software
Sell products	Guide users through ecommerce pages or upsells
Deliver content	Send PDFs, video links, tips, or discounts
Collect feedback	Run post-purchase or post-service surveys

When set up well, a chatbot becomes a **silent salesperson** that never sleeps—and businesses will pay for that.

No-Code Chatbot Platforms to Use

- **Tidio** – Fast, visual chatbot builder for ecommerce and service-based businesses
- **ManyChat** – Best for Instagram/Facebook automation and lead funnels
- **Landbot** – Beautiful conversational flows, web-based or WhatsApp integration
- **Chatfuel** – Focused on Messenger bots
- **Botpress** – Open-source platform with natural language features
- **Zapier + ChatGPT** – Custom chatbot-like workflows for niche cases

Most of these platforms have drag-and-drop builders, templates, and free starter plans.

What You Can Offer as a Chatbot Creator

Service	Deliverables	Price Range
Simple FAQ bot	5–10 answers + setup	$100–$300
Lead generation bot	Script + integration	$250–$750
Ecommerce assistant	Product recommendations, upsell flows	$400–$1,000
Booking assistant	Calendly + email flow bot	$200–$500
Custom chatbot funnel	Fully branded, multi-step funnel	$750–$2,000+

You can upsell analytics reports, script updates, and monthly management.

How to Start Building Chatbots

Step 1: Choose a use case

Start simple—FAQs for a fitness coach, booking for a salon, or lead qualification for a real estate agent.

Step 2: Use ChatGPT to write the script

Prompt:

"Create a friendly chatbot script for a local gym that welcomes new visitors, asks for their fitness goals, and offers a free trial link."

Step 3: Build the bot

Choose Tidio, Landbot, or ManyChat. Use their visual flow builder to create the conversation tree. Test it on yourself. Adjust tone and timing.

Step 4: Pitch or list your service

Options:

- Local service businesses (DMs or cold emails)
- Upwork, Fiverr, Freelancer.com
- Facebook Groups for coaches, service providers, consultants

Why This Is a High-Value Skill

- Most business owners don't know where to start with bots

- You're not selling "tech"—you're selling **time saved, leads captured, sales increased**

- You can charge recurring fees for hosting, updating, and optimizing

With AI-enhanced chatbots, you don't just help businesses respond—you help them grow automatically.

◈ Reflection & Action: Chapter 18 – Building Chatbots for Businesses

Reflect:

1. Which types of businesses in your area or network could benefit from a simple chatbot?
2. What kind of chatbot would you enjoy building—FAQ, lead capture, appointment scheduling, ecommerce assistant, or something else?
3. How could you position chatbot setup as a time-saving, income-boosting service instead of just a "tech thing"?

Journal Prompt:

_"If I helped one business grow with a chatbot, it would be a ________ that helps them ______."

Take Action:

◈ 1. Pick a Chatbot Niche + Platform

Choose a specific type of bot (lead gen, appointment, ecommerce) and pair it with a tool like:

- **Tidio** – Great for small business and ecommerce

- **ManyChat** – Ideal for coaches, influencers, Instagram-based sales

- **Landbot** – Perfect for beautifully branded flows on websites

◈ **2. Create a Sample Bot for Practice**

- Write a simple 5-message flow using **ChatGPT**

- Build it using a free account on Tidio or Landbot

- Test it on yourself and refine it until smooth

◈ **3. Create a Bot Demo Page or Video**

Record a quick Loom or screen capture video walking through your chatbot in action. Use it to pitch potential clients.

◈ **4. Offer a "Starter Bot Build" Package**

Post in a small biz group, on LinkedIn, or via DM:

"I'm offering 2 free chatbot setups for small business owners looking to capture more leads or book more appointments—DM me to claim one!"

Power Quote:

"Chatbots aren't replacing humans—they're empowering businesses to scale without burnout."

— David Moore

Chapter 19: Selling Courses Created with AI

Teach Once, Earn Forever

Online courses are one of the most powerful forms of digital income. Once created, a good course can:

- Generate sales 24/7
- Position you as an expert
- Build a community
- Lead to coaching, consulting, or product sales

And now, thanks to AI, you can go from idea to finished course in **a fraction of the time** it used to take.

Whether you want to teach marketing, mindset, meal prepping, or money management—this chapter will show you how to **use AI to create, package, and sell your own course.**

Why AI Is a Game-Changer for Course Creation

- **Faster ideation:** Brainstorm titles, lessons, and audience needs
- **Smarter structure:** AI outlines courses in logical, digestible formats
- **Easier scripting:** Generate lesson scripts, intros, and quizzes

- **Better branding:** Write headlines, bios, and ad copy in minutes
- **No editing overwhelm:** Tools like Descript and Pictory simplify production

You focus on the value—**AI handles the heavy lifting.**

Step-by-Step: Create Your Course with AI

Step 1: Choose a Clear, Solvable Problem

Your course should promise a transformation like:

- "How to start a print-on-demand shop in 30 days"
- "Write your first ebook with AI"
- "Meal plan and prep for busy moms in 1 hour/week"

Step 2: Use ChatGPT to Outline the Course

Prompt:

"Outline a 5-module online course teaching [your topic]. Each module should include 3 lessons and one takeaway exercise."

Refine. Expand. Add personal stories or insights to make it yours.

Step 3: Script Each Lesson with AI

Prompt:

"Write a 500-word lesson explaining [Lesson Title] to a beginner. Make it conversational and actionable."

Repeat for each section. Then polish for clarity and tone.

Step 4: Record or Convert to Content

Options:

- Record yourself teaching via Loom or Zoom

- Use **Synthesia** for AI avatar video delivery
- Use **Pictory** to convert text into video with visuals
- Create slide decks with **Tome** or **Canva** for self-paced learning

Step 5: Host It
Platforms to use:

- **Teachable** – Clean, beginner-friendly
- **Thinkific** – Great for community and upsells
- **Podia** – Includes email marketing and downloads
- **Gumroad** – Easy checkout and digital delivery
- **Kajabi** – High-end, all-in-one platform

Course Add-Ons to Increase Value

- Printable worksheets
- Quizzes (ChatGPT can generate these!)
- Swipe files or templates
- Bonus mini-lessons or interviews
- AI toolkits and prompt packs

Bundle them together for a **higher perceived value** and easier upsells.

Pricing Tips

Type	Price Range	Best Fit For
Mini-course	$9–$49	New audience, lead magnet
Starter course	$50–$150	DIYers, beginners
Flagship course	$199–$499+	Serious transformation, full framework
High-ticket bundle	$500–$2,000+	Includes coaching, templates, community

Start small if you're new—but remember: **Your knowledge is valuable.**

Market Your Course

- Use AI to write 10–20 promotional tweets or LinkedIn posts
- Create reels or carousels breaking down each module
- Offer a free lead magnet (checklist, mini video, PDF) to collect emails
- Run a webinar or challenge (also scripted by AI!) to build trust and drive sales

With the right idea and a structured process, you can go from concept to course in a matter of days—not months.

And once it's built? It sells while you sleep.

◈ Reflection & Action: Chapter 19 – Selling Courses Created with AI

Reflect:

1. What topic do people often ask you for advice about—or what skill could you teach confidently with a little structure and help?
2. What transformation could your ideal student achieve by the end of your course?
3. How could AI simplify the hardest part of course creation for you—outlining, scripting, recording, or promoting?

Journal Prompt:
_"If I launched a course using AI, the title would be _______ and it would help people ______."

Take Action:

◈ 1. Define Your Course Concept

Fill in this sentence:

"I want to help [who] go from [where they are now] to [the result they want] in [#] weeks."

Example: "I help beginner creators go from idea to first product in 14 days using AI."

◈ 2. Use ChatGPT to Outline Your Course

Prompt:

"Outline a 5-module course that teaches [your topic] to [your audience], with 3 lessons per module and a final outcome."

Refine the flow. Save it as your curriculum.

◈ 3. Create 1 Sample Lesson

- Use ChatGPT to script it
- Use Canva or Tome to design a slide deck

- Use Loom to record it (or Pictory to turn it into a narrated video)

⟐ 4. Choose a Hosting Platform

Test a free account on:

- Teachable
- Thinkific
- Gumroad
- Podia

Upload your content and begin collecting emails or preorders.

⟐ Bonus:

Share your course outline publicly and ask for feedback—this builds anticipation and helps shape your final offer.

Power Quote:

"Courses don't make you an expert. They prove that you're willing to share what you've already learned—and lead others through it."

— David Moore

Chapter 20: Local Lead Generation with AI Tools

Help Businesses Get Customers—on Autopilot

No matter how flashy the online world becomes, one truth remains:

Local businesses need leads to survive.

From plumbers and personal trainers to yoga studios and med spas, the biggest pain point isn't creating content—it's getting more clients through the door.

If you can use AI to help local businesses generate leads, book appointments, or capture emails, you can build a **lucrative service business** with high demand and low competition.

What Makes Local Lead Gen So Profitable

- **Small businesses often don't have in-house marketing help**
- **They'll gladly pay for predictable results** (leads, calls, bookings)
- **AI makes outreach, content, and automation faster and cheaper**
- **You can use the same system across many industries**

Lead generation isn't about making things look good—it's about **making the phone ring.**

The Local Lead Gen Funnel (AI-Enhanced)

Step 1: Capture Attention

- Use ChatGPT to write short-form ads (Google, Facebook, Instagram)
- Use Canva to design local-friendly visuals (e.g., "Free First Class!")

Step 2: Landing Page

- Use Carrd, Systeme.io, or Leadpages
- Use AI to write headline, benefits, call-to-action, and form prompts

Step 3: Collect Info

- Use forms or chatbot builders to capture names, emails, phone numbers
- Offer a simple lead magnet: discount, free consult, checklist, or sample

Step 4: Automate Follow-Up

- Use Zapier + ChatGPT + Gmail to send emails
- Use ManyChat or Tidio to auto-reply with booking links
- Schedule SMS follow-ups with tools like GoHighLevel

Niches That Need AI-Powered Lead Generation

Niche	Lead Type	Possible Offer
Fitness coaches	Consults or trial classes	"Get your first 3 sessions FREE"
Dental offices	New patient bookings	"Free whitening for new clients"
Real estate agents	Buyer/seller leads	"Get your home's value in 60 seconds"
Med spas	Beauty consultations	"$50 gift card for first-time visitors"
Auto shops	Repair quotes	"Free brake inspection + bonus checklist"
Home services	Estimate requests	"Get a same-day quote from our team"

Each of these can become a **monthly retainer client**—$500 to $2,000+ depending on results.

Tools to Build Your AI Lead Machine

- **ChatGPT** – For scripts, ad copy, and follow-up emails
- **Tidio or Landbot** – For chatbot-based lead capture
- **GoHighLevel** – All-in-one CRM, SMS/email follow-ups, automation
- **Carrd + Zapier** – Fast landing pages with simple integrations
- **Canva** – Local-friendly ads and banners

- **Google Ads + Meta Ads** – For traffic (optional, but powerful)

How to Get Clients

1. Offer a Free Mini Funnel

Reach out to 5 local businesses. Say:

"I help local [business type] get more qualified leads using smart automation and AI tools. Want me to set up a free test funnel for you?"

2. Use Local Networks

- Facebook groups
- LinkedIn (search by city + title)
- In-person BNI groups, Chamber of Commerce events

3. Start with Results, Not Features

Don't say "I'll set up automation tools."

Say:

"I'll help you get 5–10 qualified leads every week without hiring anyone."

AI makes local lead gen easier, faster, and more scalable than ever.

Your clients don't need dashboards or data—they need **customers.**

You bring them the leads, and they'll keep bringing you the business.

◈ Reflection & Action: Chapter 20 – Local Lead Generation with AI Tools

Reflect:

1. What types of local businesses do you admire, frequent, or already have relationships with?
2. How could you use AI to help a business owner capture leads, automate follow-up, or schedule more calls?
3. What fears (tech, rejection, pricing) are keeping you from offering this high-value service?

Journal Prompt:

"If I helped just one local business with AI-powered lead generation, I'd start with _______ and use _______ to deliver results."

Take Action:

◈ 1. Pick a Niche + Funnel Idea

Example:

- Niche: Barbershops
- Funnel: "Book your first cut online and get a free upgrade"

◈ 2. Build a Test Funnel Using AI Tools

- Use **ChatGPT** to write landing page copy
- Use **Carrd** to build a simple form-based landing page
- Use **Zapier** or **Tidio** to automate follow-up emails or chat replies

◈ 3. Reach Out to Local Businesses

Send this message to 3–5 small businesses near you:

"Hey [Name], I help local businesses like yours get more appointments and leads with AI-powered mini-funnels. Want me to build one for free to show you what's possible?"

◈ **Bonus:**

Track leads captured during your test run. Use screenshots or data in a simple before-and-after case study to pitch future clients.

Power Quote:

"If you can bring a business more leads, you'll never be out of work."
— David Moore

Chapter 21: AI in Stock Market Trading

The New Age of Smarter Investing

The stock market used to be dominated by Wall Street insiders and analysts with supercomputers. But today, retail traders, small investors, and solopreneurs are using **AI-powered tools** to analyze trends, scan headlines, and even build custom trading strategies—without needing a degree in finance.

This chapter explores how you can use AI to **enhance your trading, build smarter portfolios, or even sell tools and insights to others.**

What AI Can Do for Traders

Function	AI Application
Trend detection	Identify patterns in stock charts using machine learning
Sentiment analysis	Scan news and social media for bullish/bearish signals
Backtesting	Simulate trading strategies with historical data
Portfolio optimization	Adjust asset mix using predictive analytics
Trading bots	Automate buy/sell decisions using algorithms
Market summaries	Get fast, human-readable breakdowns of complex data

AI doesn't replace strategy—it **augments decision-making** with speed and objectivity.

Popular AI-Powered Tools for Traders

For Research & Analysis:

- **Finchat.io** – Ask ChatGPT-style questions about stock fundamentals
- **Kavout** – AI stock ranking and predictive scoring
- **StockGPT** – Search and summarize company earnings calls
- **Seeking Alpha + Bard/Gemini** – Blend market commentary with AI analysis

For Trading & Automation:

- **Trade Ideas** – Real-time market scanners powered by AI
- **TuringTrader** – Backtest and run algorithmic strategies
- **MetaTrader 5 + custom bots** – For Forex, crypto, and equities
- **FinRL / Alpaca** – Build AI bots if you're more technical

For Sentiment & Alerts:

- **MarketMuse + ChatGPT** – Summarize financial headlines
- **AltIndex** – Analyze alternative data like Reddit or Twitter buzz
- **Yahoo Finance + Zapier** – Create custom stock alerts based on AI input

Ways to Make Money with AI in the Market

Strategy	Skill Level	Potential
Use AI for smarter investing	Beginner	Grow your portfolio, reduce risk
Sell AI-generated market summaries	Intermediate	Newsletter, subscription, or substack model
Build trading bots or alerts	Advanced	Rent access, charge monthly
Partner with traders to optimize strategies	Intermediate	Consultant model
Create YouTube or TikTok content	Beginner	Monetize through ads, affiliate links, courses

You don't need to be a day trader. You just need to be curious, consistent, and **willing to test AI-powered insights.**

Getting Started Safely

1. Choose your market

Stocks, crypto, options, Forex—pick one lane and learn how it moves.

2. Use AI tools for research first

Don't automate trades on day one. Start with:

- Trend reports
- Company summaries
- Technical analysis helpers
- Sentiment snapshots

3. Paper trade before real money

Use tools like TradingView, Thinkorswim, or Webull's simulator to test your strategies with fake money before risking capital.

4. Create a repeatable system

Document your AI workflow:

- What tools do you check daily?
- What criteria trigger a trade or a hold?
- What emotions affect your decisions?

AI is a co-pilot—not a fortune teller. Use it to stay sharp, not reckless.

◈ Reflection & Action: Chapter 21 – AI in Stock Market Trading

Reflect:

1. What type of investor are you currently—curious beginner, casual dabbler, or active trader?
2. How could AI help you make more informed, consistent, or less emotional trading decisions?
3. Are you more interested in using AI for personal investing or creating a service/tool others can use?

Journal Prompt:

_"If I used AI to improve my trading strategy, I would focus on ________ to make decisions based on ______."

Take Action:

◈ 1. Explore One AI Trading Tool Today

Choose one tool and spend 15 minutes testing it:

- **Finchat.io** – Ask AI for stock breakdowns
- **AltIndex** – Analyze stock sentiment from social media
- **TradingView + ChatGPT** – Look at charts and get AI commentary
- **TuringTrader** – Backtest a strategy idea

◈ 2. Create a Daily AI Trading Routine
Write a checklist like:

- "Check sentiment on AltIndex"
- "Ask ChatGPT for top news summaries"
- "Use Finchat to scan 3 tickers"

Start building consistency, even with fake money.

◈ 3. Start a Market Summary Series (Optional)
Use ChatGPT to generate quick stock breakdowns and post them:

- On LinkedIn
- On Twitter
- As a Substack newsletter
- On TikTok as 60-second "AI Market Recaps"

This positions you as someone who uses tech smartly—while creating content that can later be monetized.

Power Quote:

"AI won't predict the market for you—but it will make you the most prepared person in the room."

— David Moore

Chapter 22: Crypto and AI – Risk and Reward

Where Code Meets Coin

Cryptocurrency has created overnight millionaires, launched global debates, and introduced a new financial language—but it's also become a noisy, confusing space for newcomers.

Now, AI is entering the world of crypto—not just to help you trade smarter, but to **build tools, forecast trends, analyze data, and even launch AI-integrated blockchain products.**

Whether you're a crypto-curious beginner or a DeFi fanatic, this chapter explores how you can use AI to make money in the crypto space—**while understanding the risks that come with it.**

Why AI + Crypto = Opportunity

- Crypto is data-rich → AI thrives on data
- Markets move fast → AI catches trends early
- Emotions kill trades → AI brings logic and automation
- New tools emerge daily → People need help navigating them

The synergy of AI and crypto creates powerful potential—but only for those who treat it **strategically**, not emotionally.

AI Use Cases in Crypto

Use Case	AI Application
Price prediction	ML models trained on technical indicators & sentiment
Trading bots	Auto-buy/sell based on pre-set signals
Sentiment analysis	Monitor Reddit, Twitter, Telegram trends
Portfolio optimization	Diversify assets based on AI logic
Project vetting	Use LLMs to scan whitepapers for red flags
NFT value tracking	Predict future performance based on history and hype
Content creation	Auto-write coin breakdowns, YouTube scripts, newsletters

Tools & Platforms That Combine AI + Crypto

For Trading & Prediction:

- **3Commas** – Create AI-enhanced trading bots
- **Coinrule** – Build rule-based strategies with AI templates
- **Token Metrics** – AI crypto rating and forecasting
- **Numerai** – Data scientists use AI to trade with crowd-sourced models
- **CryptoHopper** – Visual bot builder with signal marketplace

For Research & Automation:

- **ChatGPT + CoinMarketCap** – Create watchlists, summaries, and forecasts
- **Glassnode + Bard** – Analyze on-chain data and trends
- **Dune + LLMs** – Visualize and explain Ethereum data
- **Prompt engineering** – Build DeFi or NFT explainer bots

Ways to Make Money Using AI in Crypto

Method	What You Do	Risk Level
AI-assisted trading	Run or rent bots, automate swing trades	Medium to High
AI crypto newsletters	Use GPT to summarize trends, grow an audience	Low
Build NFT analysis tools	AI ranks rarity/value, sells reports or subscriptions	Medium
Build bots for others	Sell setup as a freelance service	Low to Medium
AI + DeFi tutorials	Create courses or guides	Low
Prompt packs for crypto traders	Sell cheat sheets for bot building or investing	Low

Key Cautions and Realities

- **AI doesn't eliminate risk**—it just helps manage it
- **Bots can crash markets just as fast as they enter them**

- **Garbage in, garbage out**—a poorly trained model can lose money fast
- **Regulation is coming**—know the rules before offering financial products
- **Don't blindly trust "AI prediction platforms" without verifying their models**

Crypto is volatile. AI can help—but **you are still responsible for your decisions.**

How to Start

1. **Choose your lane**: Trader, researcher, content creator, tool builder
2. **Pick 2–3 tools to master**: Try Coinrule, ChatGPT, and Token Metrics
3. **Test with play money**: Simulate or use small trades before going big
4. **Document everything**: Whether you're building bots or writing breakdowns, turn your work into assets (courses, posts, freelance gigs)

The future of finance is being written in **code + prompts.**

If you understand both—**you can create value in any market condition.**

◈ Reflection & Action: Chapter 22 – Crypto and AI: Risk and Reward

Reflect:

1. What is your current relationship with cryptocurrency—investor, observer, skeptic, or enthusiast?
2. Which aspect of AI in crypto intrigues you most: trading bots, NFT analytics, sentiment tracking, or content creation?
3. How can you start experimenting with AI in crypto **without putting your finances at major risk**?

Journal Prompt:
"The safest and smartest way I can explore AI in crypto is by ________ while using tools like ________ to learn and track progress."

Take Action:

◈ 1. Choose One Focus Area to Explore

Pick one low-risk entry point:

- Create an AI-generated newsletter summarizing daily crypto news
- Use Token Metrics or ChatGPT to research promising coins
- Analyze sentiment on a favorite coin using Reddit/Twitter + LLM tools
- Build a demo trading bot using Coinrule or CryptoHopper with test funds

◈ 2. Build Your Personal Crypto AI Stack

List the tools you'll use this month. Example:

- **ChatGPT** – Ask questions, summarize coin trends
- **3Commas** – Build and monitor a safe trading bot
- **Glassnode** – Analyze Bitcoin and Ethereum on-chain data
- **CoinMarketCap** – Build a custom AI watchlist

◈ 3. Set a Testing Budget and Time Frame

Create a "learning wallet" with $50–$100 (or paper trade only).

Give yourself 30 days to experiment, track wins/losses, and decide if it's worth scaling.

◈ Bonus:

Document your journey via social media, a blog, or YouTube.

Even your beginner-level insights can attract an audience—and income.

Power Quote:

"In crypto and in AI, the winners are the ones who learn fast, move smart, and stay humble."

— David Moore

Chapter 23: Selling AI Services on Freelance Platforms

Monetize Your AI Skills Without Building a Business

Not everyone wants to launch a brand or build a product. Some of us want to **make money now** by offering valuable services—and that's where freelancing comes in.

With AI at your side, you don't need to be an expert designer, developer, or writer. You just need to know how to deliver solutions faster and better than the next freelancer.

This chapter shows how to **sell AI-powered services** on platforms like **Fiverr, Upwork, PeoplePerHour, and Freelancer.com**, using tools like ChatGPT, Midjourney, and more.

Why Freelance + AI = Fast Cashflow

- You can start today—with no followers, no email list, and no product
- Clients care about **results**, not how you made them
- AI cuts your delivery time by 70–90%
- You can offer services that look custom, but are powered by repeatable systems
- You get paid to practice your skills and refine your niche

This is one of the **fastest paths to income with AI**—especially for solopreneurs, students, or career switchers.

Freelance Services You Can Offer With AI

Service	AI Tools	Estimated Rate
Blog post writing	ChatGPT, Jasper	$30–$150/post
Logo & branding	Midjourney, Canva	$50–$300
Video editing & captions	Pictory, Descript	$100–$500/video
Social media content	ChatGPT, Canva	$100–$300/mo
Resume & cover letter writing	ChatGPT, Resume.io	$40–$150/package
Product descriptions	ChatGPT	$10–$30/ description
AI chatbot setup	Tidio, Landbot	$150–$750
Voiceovers	ElevenLabs	$20–$100/min
YouTube scripts	ChatGPT, Claude	$30–$200/script

Start with what you can confidently deliver—and let AI help you **overdeliver**.

How to Get Started (Fast)

1. Pick 1-2 services

Choose based on your interest + ease of delivery. If you enjoy writing, scripting, or visual design, you're already ahead.

2. Create a high-converting profile

Use ChatGPT to write:

- Your Fiverr or Upwork bio
- Gig descriptions with clear outcomes
- Sample project titles (e.g., "I will write 1000-word SEO blog posts using AI")

3. Build a sample portfolio
Even if you've never had clients, use AI to create:

- 3 blog post samples
- 2 logo mockups
- 1 chatbot demo
- 1 video clip

4. Start pitching and applying

- Apply to 5+ gigs per day on Upwork
- List 3–5 Fiverr gigs with variations
- Post your samples on LinkedIn and Facebook groups
- DM small businesses or solopreneurs offering a "free sample" or "discounted first gig"

How to Stand Out

- Emphasize speed + value ("Delivered in 48 hours using smart AI tools")
- Show proof (before/after, testimonials, screenshots)
- Offer bonuses (extra revisions, additional formats, one-week support)
- Be client-centric—not tool-centric. Say:

"I'll write engaging product descriptions that increase conversions,"

not

"I'll use ChatGPT to write stuff."

Scaling Your Freelance Income

- Turn services into **packages** (e.g., $300/mo for 4 blog posts + SEO titles)
- Build **repeat clients** by offering monthly deals
- Raise prices once you've completed 10+ jobs
- **Outsource** work using AI or junior freelancers
- Teach your process and sell it as a **course or coaching** later

You don't need to be a guru. You just need to **be useful, consistent, and AI-enhanced.**

⟐ Reflection & Action: Chapter 23 – Selling AI Services on Freelance Platforms

Reflect:

1. What service do you feel confident offering right now—writing, design, editing, or strategy?
2. How could AI help you deliver that service **faster, cheaper, or with higher quality** than the average freelancer?
3. What's stopping you from creating your first freelance gig today?

Journal Prompt:

_"My most valuable skill right now is _______. I could start offering it on Fiverr or Upwork by using AI to help me ______."

Take Action:

◈ 1. Choose Your Starter Service

Decide what you're going to offer. Examples:

- "I'll write SEO blog posts using AI."
- "I'll design logos using Midjourney + Canva."
- "I'll create AI chatbots for small business websites."

◈ 2. Use ChatGPT to Build Your First Gig

Prompt:

"Write a Fiverr gig description for someone offering [your service] using AI tools. Include a title, short description, and 3 package levels."

◈ 3. Create a Sample Project

- Write a 500-word blog post with ChatGPT
- Design 2 logos in Midjourney and present them in Canva
- Record a short YouTube script or social media post

◈ 4. Upload Your Gig and Start Pitching

- List it on Fiverr or Upwork
- Post it on LinkedIn with a simple caption like:

"I'm now offering fast, affordable AI-powered [service] for creators and small businesses. DM me if you want to test it out!"

◈ Bonus:

Do your first few gigs for free or discounted in exchange for testimonials and reviews. This builds momentum.

Power Quote:
"Freelancing is freedom—but AI makes it frictionless."
— David Moore

Chapter 24: Writing & Selling AI-Powered eBooks

Turn Words Into Wealth—Faster Than Ever

Writing a book used to take months—sometimes years. Now, with the help of AI, you can go from idea to published eBook in **a matter of days**.

The key isn't just using AI to write—it's knowing how to guide it, refine it, format it, and **turn it into something people actually want to buy**.

In this chapter, you'll learn how to use ChatGPT and other tools to create, publish, and sell eBooks that generate income long after you've hit "export."

Why eBooks Still Work

- **Low barrier to entry**—no publisher or massive audience needed
- **Passive income potential**—sell while you sleep
- **Establishes credibility**—useful for coaches, freelancers, creators
- **Bundles well**—with courses, services, or subscriptions
- **Repurposable**—turn chapters into blog posts, reels, tweets, and videos

With the right topic and structure, your eBook becomes an **automated income and credibility builder.**

Step-by-Step: Create an AI-Powered eBook

Step 1: Pick a Profitable Topic

Look for:

- Pain points ("How to fix..." "How to overcome...")
- Desires ("How to build..." "How to achieve...")
- Curiosity ("Secrets of..." "Truth about...")

Hot niches:

- AI and tech
- Side hustles
- Health and fitness
- Relationships
- Mindset and productivity
- Personal finance
- Parenting hacks
- Creative writing guides

Step 2: Outline with ChatGPT

Prompt:

"Outline a 10-chapter eBook about [your topic] that helps [target reader] solve [core problem]."

Refine the structure, add personal insights or case studies, and use bullet points if needed.

Step 3: Write the First Draft

Prompt:

"Write Chapter 1 of the above eBook. Make it friendly, actionable, and 800–1,000 words long."

Continue chapter by chapter. Use your voice to edit and improve each draft.

Step 4: Format and Design

Use:

- **Atticus** or **Reedsy** – for clean eBook formatting
- **Canva** – for a high-converting cover
- **Vellum** – if you're on Mac and want pro formatting

Step 5: Publish & Sell

Platforms:

- **Amazon KDP** – The biggest eBook marketplace in the world
- **Gumroad** – Great for direct sales
- **Payhip** – Clean and creator-friendly
- **Shopify + Email list** – Build a brand around your book

Price Points That Work

Type	Length	Price
Short guide	20–30 pages	\$5–\$9
Standard eBook	40–100 pages	\$9–\$19
Premium guide	100+ pages + extras	\$20–\$49
Bundle (eBook + video + bonus)	Any	\$50–\$199

Start small, validate demand, then add more value and raise the price.

Promotion Made Easy with AI

- Use ChatGPT to generate:
  - 10 social media posts
  - Email launch sequence
  - Book description (Amazon or Gumroad)
  - Ads, captions, and even review requests
- Use **Pictory** to turn chapters into video
- Use **Reels + Carousels** on Instagram to pull quotes and tips

Your book becomes a **content engine** and a product all in one.

> You don't need to be a bestselling author.
> You just need to **solve a problem clearly and offer it proudly.**

⟐ Reflection & Action: Chapter 24 – Writing & Selling AI-Powered eBooks

Reflect:

1. What is one problem you've overcome or skill you've mastered that others constantly ask you about?
2. What kind of eBook could you write in 10 chapters using AI to draft and organize your thoughts?
3. Would you prefer to sell your book on Amazon, your own website, or both?

Journal Prompt:

_"If I published an eBook this month, it would be called _______ and it would help people ______."

Take Action:

⟐ 1. Brainstorm Your Topic

Ask ChatGPT:

"What are 10 eBook topics in the [your niche] space that solve urgent problems or offer quick wins?"

Pick the one that excites you **and** feels helpful to others.

⟐ 2. Generate a Chapter-by-Chapter Outline

Prompt:

"Outline a 10-chapter eBook about [your topic] for [your audience]. Each chapter should teach one concept or step."

⟐ 3. Draft Your First Chapter with ChatGPT

Prompt:

"Write Chapter 1 of the above eBook. Keep it under 1,000 words, conversational, and include examples."

⟐ 4. Design a Cover in Canva

Search for "eBook Cover" templates, drop in your title and author name, and download a polished version.

◈ 5. Publish and Promote

Upload your eBook to:

- **Amazon KDP** for wide reach
- **Gumroad or Payhip** for direct sales
- **Your own site** with email opt-ins and bonuses

Power Quote:

"Your eBook doesn't have to be perfect—it just has to be useful. And now, with AI, it can be both."

— David Moore

Chapter 25: Creating & Monetizing AI Art

Turn Prompts Into Profits

Art isn't just for galleries anymore—it's for merch, marketing, book covers, gaming assets, and even NFTs. And thanks to AI, you no longer need to be a master illustrator to create stunning visuals that people will pay for.

Whether you're a creative entrepreneur or just curious about design, this chapter will show you how to **use AI art tools to generate, sell, and profit from digital artwork.**

Why AI Art is a Growing Opportunity

- You can create art **fast**—minutes instead of hours
- Clients care about **results**, not how the image was made
- There's demand for everything from logos to wallpapers to t-shirt designs
- AI lets **non-artists** explore creative business models
- You can sell the same image in **multiple formats** to multiple buyers

Top Tools for AI Art Creation

Tool	Use Case
Midjourney	High-quality, stylized AI illustrations
DALL·E 3	Realistic and accurate text-to-image generation
Leonardo.ai	Game assets, fantasy, and stylized design
Canva + AI	Posters, social posts, and products with AI integration
NightCafe / Dream by Wombo	NFT art and abstract style generation
Runway ML	Turn images into videos or animations

Combine tools to get the look, scale, and format you need.

Ways to Make Money With AI Art

Method	What You Do	Where to Sell
Print-on-demand	Create t-shirt, mug, phone case designs	Redbubble, TeePublic, Etsy
Stock image licensing	Upload AI art as stock photos	Adobe Stock, Creative Market
Book covers & album art	Niche custom artwork for creators	Fiverr, Upwork, direct clients
Wallpapers & digital packs	Themed sets (fantasy, cyberpunk, minimalist)	Gumroad, Etsy
NFT collections	Unique art drops with scarcity model	OpenSea, Rarible
Coloring books or posters	Bundle AI illustrations as printable products	Amazon KDP, Teachers Pay Teachers
Custom AI portraits	Fantasy, pet, or pop culture-inspired commissions	Instagram, Shopify

Your art becomes **an asset**—something that earns again and again.

How to Create Art That Sells

1. Pick a Niche

Fantasy, cyberpunk, spiritual, abstract, retro, anime, minimalism—niches sell.

2. Study What's Trending

Use Etsy, Redbubble, or Behance to explore popular searches. Example:

"Vaporwave cat poster"

"Witchcore coloring pages"

"Afrofuturist digital wallpaper set"

3. Write a Precise Prompt

Prompt example for Midjourney:

"Highly detailed surreal landscape with neon crystals, floating islands, cinematic lighting — 16:9"

4. Generate, Refine, Upscale

- Use multiple variations
- Upscale best results
- Edit or format in Canva or Photoshop

5. Package It

Turn a single image into:

- Poster
- Wallpaper
- Sticker set

- Coloring page
- Mockup display

One idea. **Five+ products.**

Bonus: Sell AI Art as a Service

- "I'll design a unique fantasy book cover"
- "Custom pet portraits in a vaporwave style"
- "Create YouTube thumbnail art with Midjourney"
- "AI-generated tattoo concept based on your idea"

AI + creativity = an **endless product line.**

You don't have to be an artist to sell art.
You just need **vision, good prompts, and smart packaging.**

◈ Reflection & Action: Chapter 25 – Creating & Monetizing AI Art

Reflect:

1. What kind of visual art or design has always caught your attention—fantasy, fashion, spiritual, sci-fi, minimalist, pop culture?
2. How could you use AI to create artwork that speaks to that interest or style?
3. Would you rather **sell digital downloads**, offer a **custom art service**, or **license your art**?

Journal Prompt:

_"If I created a line of AI-generated art, the theme would be ________ and I'd sell it as _______."

Take Action:

◈ 1. Choose Your Art Niche

Browse Etsy or Redbubble and pick a profitable theme:

- Afrofuturism
- Witchcore
- Retro minimalism
- Streetwear graphic design
- Cute animal patterns
- Cyberpunk fantasy

◈ 2. Create Your First Prompt in Midjourney or DALL·E

Prompt:

"A bold, futuristic Afrocentric queen with glowing gold accessories, cinematic lighting, Afro-punk style — 4K, digital painting, highly detailed."

◈ 3. Turn It Into a Product

Download and repurpose your artwork into:

- Printable wall art
- Phone wallpapers
- T-shirt mockups
- Instagram carousels

- Poster sets on Canva

◈ **4. Choose Your Marketplace**

- **Etsy** – Printables, merch, digital downloads
- **Redbubble / TeePublic** – POD designs
- **Gumroad** – Wallpaper packs, coloring books
- **Fiverr** – Custom commissions
- **Creative Market** – Stock image bundles

◈ **Bonus:**

Use ChatGPT to write your product listings, titles, and SEO-optimized descriptions to increase visibility and conversion.

Power Quote:

"You don't need to draw to be an artist anymore. You just need vision—and the right tools."

— David Moore

Chapter 26: Building AI-Powered Websites and Landing Pages

Sell Smarter, Faster, and Cleaner With AI

In the digital economy, a clean, persuasive website is often the difference between getting a sale and getting ignored. But most people don't know how to code—and hiring designers and copywriters can get expensive fast.

That's where AI comes in.

With the right tools and prompts, you can **build high-converting landing pages, full websites, and branded micro-sites** using AI—even if you've never written a line of HTML in your life.

And best of all? You can build them **for your own products** or as a **freelance service** for others.

Why AI Web Creation Is a Goldmine

- No coding required
- Launch in hours, not weeks
- Copy, images, and layout generated with a few clicks
- Small businesses will **gladly pay** for beautiful, fast, affordable websites
- You can use the same formula again and again with different clients

Tools for AI-Powered Website Creation

Tool	What It Does
Durable.co	Creates full business websites with AI in 30 seconds
10Web.io	WordPress AI builder with drag-and-drop simplicity
Unbounce + ChatGPT	AI-written landing pages for marketing & sales
Wix AI Builder	Walks you through creation with smart suggestions
Webflow + Relume	Build beautiful sites with AI-generated sections
Copy.ai / Jasper / ChatGPT	Writes site copy, headlines, CTAs, and form text
Canva	Design graphics and mockups for each section

These tools replace the need for coders and agencies—for a fraction of the cost.

Pages That Clients Need (or You Can Build for Yourself)

Page Type	Who Needs It
Landing page	Coaches, consultants, product launches
Link-in-bio page	Creators, influencers, small biz owners
Lead magnet opt-in	Marketers, authors, podcasters
Product sales page	E-commerce, digital products
Personal portfolio	Freelancers, artists, writers
Booking form	Fitness, wellness, local services
Mini-site	Event pages, challenges, one-page resumes

You only need 1–2 pages to start monetizing.

How to Build Your First AI Website

Step 1: Choose a Client or Concept

- Yourself: Portfolio, ebook, product
- Local biz: Gym, therapist, tutor
- Offer to a friend or peer for free to get experience

Step 2: Use ChatGPT to Write the Copy

Prompt:

"Write a homepage headline, subheadline, three benefit bullets, and a strong CTA for a [business type] helping [audience] solve [problem]."

Step 3: Choose Your Platform

- Durable or 10Web for all-in-one solutions
- Webflow if you want pro-level design control
- Carrd for dead-simple, beautiful one-pagers

Step 4: Generate Visuals

- Canva: Logos, banners, icons
- Midjourney: Backgrounds or stylized brand art
- Pexels / Unsplash: Free, high-quality photos

Step 5: Publish + Promote

- Connect a custom domain
- Use social media, email, and SEO keywords to drive traffic
- List your services on Fiverr, Upwork, or niche directories

Freelance Pricing Potential

Service	Rate Range
Single-page website	$150–$500
Landing page + email form	$200–$750
Full 3–5 page site	$500–$2,500
Website + branding + copy	$1,000–$5,000
Monthly maintenance	$50–$200/mo per client

The secret? **You use AI to do 80% of the work**, but clients still see 100% of the value.

> You don't need to code to get paid.
> You just need to **build smart and deliver fast.**

◈ Reflection & Action: Chapter 26 – Building AI-Powered Websites and Landing Pages

Reflect:

1. What kind of website or landing page could you build today—with help from AI—that would either promote **your own product** or **help someone else's business grow**?
2. Do you feel more drawn to building sites for **clients, personal use**, or **digital products**?
3. How could you use AI to speed up design, content creation,

and launch?

Journal Prompt:

_"If I used AI to build a website this week, it would be for _______ and it would help _______ solve ______."

Take Action:

◈ 1. Choose a Site Type

Pick one type of page to start with:

- Personal portfolio
- eBook or product sales page
- Local business landing page
- Booking form for a coach or consultant
- Link-in-bio page for social media

◈ 2. Use ChatGPT to Generate the Copy

Prompt example:

"Write website copy for a [type of business] that helps [audience] achieve [result]. Include: headline, subheadline, 3 benefits, CTA, and short about section."

◈ 3. Build It on a No-Code AI Platform

Try:

- Durable.co[1] – 1-minute AI websites
- 10Web.io[2] – Drag-and-drop builder

---

1. https://durable.co
2. https://10web.io

- Carrd.co[3] – Beautiful one-page simplicity
- Webflow[4] – Pro-level design with AI assistance

◈ 4. Add Visuals Using AI + Canva

- Use Midjourney or DALL·E to create headers, icons, or abstract backgrounds
- Drop them into Canva to match your brand colors or layout

◈ 5. Offer Your Service to Someone Else

Pitch example:

"Hey [Name], I've started building fast, professional AI-powered websites for small business owners. Want a free draft version to check out?"

Power Quote:

"A single landing page—written and designed with AI—can make you money for years."

— David Moore

3. https://carrd.co
4. https://webflow.com

Chapter 27: Mastering Prompt Engineering for Profit

The Real Skill Behind AI Success

AI tools are only as powerful as the instructions you give them. That's why "prompt engineering" has become one of the most valuable skills in the modern digital economy.

In simple terms: **prompt engineering is the art of talking to AI in a way that gets exactly what you want.**

From writing killer ad copy to designing jaw-dropping images, mastering prompts means you **save time, stand out, and get paid more.**

In this chapter, we'll explore how to make money by:

- Writing better prompts
- Selling prompt templates
- Teaching prompt skills
- Offering done-for-you AI content generation

What Makes a Good Prompt?

A great prompt is:

- **Clear**: No ambiguity or fluff
- **Specific**: Tells AI what tone, format, and outcome you expect

- **Context-rich**: Includes relevant info, goals, and examples
- **Iterative**: Refined and tested for better results each time

Bad prompt:

"Write a blog post about fitness."

Better prompt:

"Write a friendly, 800-word blog post for beginners on how to lose weight through intermittent fasting. Include a catchy headline, subheadings, and 3 tips."

High-Income Prompt Use Cases

Use Case	Where It Pays Off
Ad copywriting	Facebook, Google, Instagram campaigns
YouTube scripts	Hook-first, storytelling-driven content
Midjourney image prompts	Book covers, merch, NFT design
Business naming	Brand identity creation
Product descriptions	Amazon, Etsy, Shopify stores
Job interview prep	Career coaching and HR services
Personalized emails	Cold outreach and follow-ups
AI course creation	Teach how to prompt, monetize it
Prompt packs	Sell templates on Gumroad or Fiverr

Tools to Practice and Refine Prompts

- **ChatGPT / Claude / Gemini** – Text generation
- **Midjourney / DALL·E / Leonardo** – Visual prompts

- **PromptHero.com** – Prompt marketplace for learning and inspiration
- **FlowGPT / AIPRM** – Curated prompt libraries
- **Prompt Engineering Guide** – Free online resource for mastering techniques

The more prompts you test and refine, the more valuable your work becomes.

How to Monetize Prompt Engineering

1. Sell Prompt Packs

- "100 ChatGPT prompts for real estate agents"
- "50 Midjourney prompts for t-shirt designers"
- "30 storytelling prompts for YouTube creators"

Sell on:

- Gumroad
- Ko-fi
- Etsy (as digital downloads)
- Your own site

2. Offer Prompt Consulting Services

- Help creators, coaches, and marketers automate content with prompts

- Example: "I'll build a prompt bank that generates 30 days of content for your brand."

3. Teach Prompting

- Launch a mini-course or ebook:

"Prompt Like a Pro: How to Get 10x More from ChatGPT"

- Offer 1-on-1 coaching or live workshops

4. Create AI-Powered Content Systems

- Build reusable prompt flows:
  - Blog writer
  - Email sequencer
  - Ad campaign builder
  - Podcast outline generator

Sell them as done-for-you services or templates.

Prompting is a **leverage skill.**
The better your prompts, the faster you create—and the more value you deliver.

◈ Reflection & Action: Chapter 27 – Mastering Prompt Engineering for Profit

Reflect:

1. What types of AI tasks do you find yourself doing often—writing, designing, scripting, branding?
2. How could better prompts make those tasks **faster, more creative, or more profitable**?
3. Would you rather use prompts to **serve clients, sell templates**, or **build your own content systems**?

Journal Prompt:

_"One niche or industry that could benefit from a prompt pack I create is _______. I could help them save time or grow faster by offering prompts for ______."

Take Action:

◈ 1. Practice Crafting Expert-Level Prompts

Try this base formula and experiment:

"Act as a [role]. Write a [format] for [audience] that achieves [goal]. Keep the tone [style]. Include [elements like bullet points, CTAs, or examples]."

Example:

"Act as a social media strategist. Write a carousel post for wellness coaches that explains how to increase Instagram engagement in 3 easy steps. Use a friendly, motivational tone and include emojis and a call to action."

◈ 2. Build a Prompt Pack Around a Specific Niche

Pick one audience—coaches, Etsy sellers, authors, teachers—and create:

- 10–50 prompts that solve real problems
- A simple PDF or Notion doc
- A short explanation or use guide

◈ 3. Sell or Share Your Pack

List it on:

- **Gumroad or Ko-fi**
- **Your social media channels**
- **Freelance marketplaces** (as a downloadable or add-on)

◈ Bonus:

Offer a free mini-pack in exchange for email sign-ups. Grow your list while building trust.

Power Quote:

"Those who master prompts will write the future—faster, clearer, and richer than ever before."

— David Moore

Chapter 28: Launching AI-Powered Courses and Coaching

Teach What You Know, Amplify It With AI

You don't need a PhD to teach anymore. You need **clarity, confidence, and content**—and AI gives you all three.

Whether you're a writer, designer, entrepreneur, or hobbyist, there's someone out there who wants to learn what you know. This chapter will show you how to use AI to **plan, produce, and profit from digital courses and coaching programs**—even if you've never taught before.

Why Courses and Coaching Are High-Income Opportunities

- You only need to create it once—then sell it over and over
- You can charge more for transformation than information
- Coaching adds a premium, human connection
- AI does the heavy lifting: outlines, slides, emails, even voiceovers
- You don't need a big audience to make a big impact

AI turns your knowledge into a **scalable, sellable product.**

Use AI to Build a Course From Scratch

Step 1: Choose Your Transformation

People don't buy information—they buy results. Ask:

"What specific result can I help someone get in 2–4 weeks?"
Examples:

- "Go from camera shy to confident on TikTok"
- "Launch your first Etsy store using AI"
- "Create a professional eBook with ChatGPT in 7 days"
- "Design a brand kit using Midjourney + Canva"

Step 2: Ask AI for a Course Outline
Prompt:
"Outline a 5-module course on [topic] that helps [target audience] go from [point A] to [point B]. Include lesson titles and outcomes."
Step 3: Generate Lesson Content
Use ChatGPT to create:

- Slide notes or scripts
- Email sequences
- Lesson quizzes
- Workbooks or checklists
- Social media promos

Step 4: Record or Deliver the Course
Choose your format:

- Pre-recorded video (using Loom, Zoom, or Descript)
- PDF slides + templates (Canva)

- Audio training
- Live Zoom workshops

Step 5: Host and Sell
Platforms:

- **Gumroad** – All-in-one for digital products
- **Teachable / Thinkific** – Full course platforms
- **Podia / Kajabi** – Great for coaching + upsells
- **Circle / Discord** – Community-led learning

Add Coaching for Higher Value

People pay more for **access + accountability.**
You can offer:

- 1:1 coaching calls ($100–$1,000+)
- Group coaching programs ($500–$5,000)
- Voxer/DM support ($50–$200/week)
- Weekly office hours or Q&A

Package examples:

- **$97** for a DIY course
- **$297** for the course + templates

- **$997** for course + weekly group coaching
- **$2,000+** for private VIP coaching + audits

Course Ideas You Can Launch in 30 Days

Skill	Course Title
Writing	"Blog in a Week With ChatGPT"
Design	"Create Viral Pinterest Pins with AI"
Marketing	"Automate Your Email List with AI Tools"
AI itself	"Prompt Mastery for Small Business Owners"
Side Hustles	"Start a Digital Product Biz With Zero Code"
Freelancing	"Land 3 Clients in 30 Days Using ChatGPT"

Start with what you've already done—and help others do the same.

> AI lets you **teach smarter, faster, and more profitably.**
> You bring the value. AI brings the engine.

◈ Reflection & Action: Chapter 28 – Launching AI-Powered Courses and Coaching

Reflect:

1. What is something you've done (or figured out) that others often ask you for help with?
2. Could that knowledge be turned into a **mini-course, paid workshop**, or **coaching offer**?
3. What transformation could you help someone achieve with a little structure and a lot of AI assistance?

Journal Prompt:

_"If I launched a course this month, it would be called _______ and it would help _______ go from _______ to ______."

Take Action:

◈ 1. Identify the Transformation You Can Offer

Ask ChatGPT:

"Help me brainstorm course titles for someone who can teach [skill] to [audience] with the goal of helping them [result]."

Example:

"Help me brainstorm course titles for someone who can teach AI art to Etsy sellers with the goal of helping them launch a store."

◈ 2. Create a 5-Module Outline

Prompt:

"Outline a 5-module course on [course title] that guides [audience] to [result]. Each module should include lessons and deliverables."

◈ 3. Choose Your Delivery Method

- PDF slides
- Screen-recorded video lessons
- Audio-only training
- Live Zoom sessions
- Pre-recorded + group coaching hybrid

◈ 4. Package and Price It

Tiered example:

- **$97** – Self-paced course only
- **$297** – Course + templates

- **$997** – Course + group coaching
- **$1,997+** – VIP coaching, audits, or 1-on-1 access

◈ 5. Promote It with AI Help

- Generate email funnels, launch pages, and testimonials with ChatGPT
- Use Midjourney or Canva to create branded course visuals
- Use social media AI tools to write carousels, reels, or tweets

Power Quote:
"You're already an expert at something—AI just helps you teach it faster, package it smarter, and sell it wider."
— David Moore

Chapter 29: Building AI Chatbots for Businesses

Automate, Engage, and Convert—24/7

Businesses are waking up to a new reality: customers expect instant answers. Whether it's booking a haircut, getting product info, or checking order status—**AI chatbots are the new frontline of customer experience.**

And that's your opportunity.

With tools like ChatGPT, ManyChat, and Botpress, you can build smart, responsive chatbots for websites, e-commerce shops, service providers, and influencers. Best of all, you don't need to code. You just need **strategy, tools, and solid prompts.**

Why Chatbots Are in Demand

- 24/7 automated support
- Collect leads and qualify buyers
- Save businesses time and staff costs
- Deliver consistent answers and upsells
- Great for local service businesses, online stores, creators, and coaches

Businesses will gladly pay for a tool that saves them time and makes them money.

Types of Chatbots You Can Build

Bot Type	Who Needs It	What It Does
Lead generation bot	Real estate agents, consultants	Captures contact info + preferences
Appointment booking bot	Barbers, dentists, tutors	Schedules sessions via calendar sync
FAQ/helpdesk bot	E-commerce, SaaS	Answers common customer questions
Sales funnel bot	Coaches, creators, course sellers	Qualifies leads, offers upsells
Instagram DM bot	Influencers, brands	Automates replies + links from comments
Welcome bot	Discord, Telegram, Slack	Onboards users, shares resources
Newsletter opt-in bot	Bloggers, podcasters	Captures emails in exchange for a freebie

Tools to Build No-Code AI Chatbots

Tool	Strength
ManyChat	Best for Facebook + Instagram DM automation
Tidio	E-commerce chatbot for Shopify, WooCommerce
Landbot.io	Drag-and-drop chatbots for websites + WhatsApp
Chatbase	Upload your docs and create a bot trained on your content
Botpress	Build advanced GPT-4 powered bots with logic
Zapier + ChatGPT API	Combine automation and AI responses

You don't need to write code—you just need to define the **goal, flow, and tone.**

How to Build a Chatbot That Works

Step 1: Choose a Business Use Case

Example: A fitness coach wants to book more consults.

Step 2: Map the Conversation Flow

Prompt:

"Create a chatbot script that welcomes new users, asks what fitness goal they have, offers a free 10-minute consult, and schedules a Zoom call."

Step 3: Build It in a Tool Like ManyChat or Landbot

- Use drag-and-drop blocks
- Plug in your AI-generated script
- Add email or calendar integrations

Step 4: Train the Bot (If Using GPT)

- Upload FAQs, product details, or PDF guides
- Connect it to ChatGPT via tools like Chatbase or Botpress
- Test and refine responses

Step 5: Embed or Link the Bot

- Add it to your client's website
- Use a link in bio

- Embed it in popups or landing pages
- Promote it via social posts, QR codes, or email

How to Monetize Your Bot-Building Skills

Offer Type	Pricing Range
Basic FAQ chatbot	$100–$300
Sales funnel bot	$300–$1,000
Full lead gen + booking bot	$750–$2,500
Monthly maintenance	$50–$200 per client
AI bot strategy session	$150/hour

Bonus: Sell chatbot templates or cloneable flows as digital products.

Businesses don't want "just a bot."

They want **conversions, time saved, and better customer experiences.**

With AI, you can deliver all three.

⍰ Reflection & Action: Chapter 29 – Building AI Chatbots for Businesses

Reflect:

1. What kind of businesses do you interact with most—coaches, stores, creators, service providers?
2. How could a chatbot save them time or help them book more clients or make more sales?
3. Do you see yourself offering chatbot services, selling templates, or using bots to boost your own business?

Journal Prompt:

"If I built a chatbot today, it would be for _______ and it would help users _______ without needing human support."

Take Action:

⟐ 1. Choose a Simple Bot Use Case

Start with one:

- Welcome + FAQ bot for a small business
- Lead generation bot for a coach or agency
- Appointment scheduler for a local service provider
- Newsletter opt-in bot offering a freebie or discount

⟐ 2. Generate the Conversation Script with AI

Prompt example:

"Write a chatbot flow for a real estate agent that welcomes users, asks for property preferences, and offers to book a free home tour."

⟐ 3. Build the Bot in a No-Code Tool

Try:

- **ManyChat** for social media DM bots
- **Landbot** for drag-and-drop web bots
- **Chatbase** to train ChatGPT on a business's content
- **Tidio** for Shopify or WooCommerce stores

⟐ 4. Test and Launch It

- Run through test conversations

- Add it to a website, landing page, or link-in-bio
- Promote it through an Instagram post or email blast

◈ 5. Offer Your Bot Services

Create a Fiverr or Upwork listing, or reach out directly to a few business owners you know and say:

"I can build a custom AI chatbot that books clients and answers FAQs—want a free demo?"

Power Quote:

"Chatbots don't just talk. They work—24/7, with zero burnout, turning visitors into customers while you sleep."

— David Moore

Chapter 30: Monetizing AI Voice and Audio Tools

Let AI Speak for You—and Pay You

We're living in a world where voices don't have to be real to feel real. AI voice and audio tools have opened up a powerful way to create audiobooks, ads, YouTube narration, podcasts, and even character voices—**without ever stepping in a studio.**

This chapter will show you how to turn AI audio into income streams by creating, editing, and selling voice-based content that sounds professional, fast.

Why Voice-Based AI Is Booming

- Audiobooks, podcasting, and video content are exploding
- People want **audio options** for blogs, training, and sales pages
- AI voices are getting **realistic and customizable**
- You can launch audio products without recording gear
- Creators and marketers need help producing fast, clean voice content

Best AI Voice & Audio Tools Right Now

Tool	Use Case
ElevenLabs	Ultra-realistic voice synthesis, custom voice cloning
Play.ht	Convert blog posts and scripts to lifelike audio
Descript	Edit podcasts and video using text + overdub voice
Lovo.ai	Voiceovers for ads, explainers, and e-learning
Murf.ai	Commercial-quality voiceovers for video creators
WellSaid Labs	Corporate-style narration with high fidelity
Revoicer	Budget-friendly AI voiceovers for beginners

Ways to Make Money With AI Audio

Offer	How It Works	Where to Sell
Audiobook narration	Convert your (or others') books into AI-narrated audio	Amazon ACX, Gumroad
Voiceover services	Ads, YouTube intros, explainer videos	Fiverr, Upwork
Podcast production	Script + voice + edit with AI	Freelance or personal brand
AI voice packs	Sell voice templates for games or content creators	Gumroad, Ko-fi
Audio summaries	Summarize blog posts or newsletters into spoken clips	Social media or client offers
Video narration	Use AI to voice TikToks, reels, YouTube shorts	Your brand or client content
Character voices	Storytelling, animation, or games	Indie creators, writers, developers

You can become a one-person audio studio using nothing but AI.

Example: Create an AI-Narrated Audiobook

1. **Write or License a Book**

• Use ChatGPT to create a short guide, story, or niche manual

• Or narrate a public domain classic (with a twist)

1. **Convert Text to Audio**

• Use ElevenLabs or Murf.ai

• Choose voice tone: calm, energetic, deep, warm, etc.

1. **Edit and Enhance**

• Use Descript to cut pauses, boost clarity

• Add light background music with royalty-free tracks

1. **Publish**

• Upload to **ACX (Audible)**, **Gumroad**, or **your website**

• Promote with AI-made ads or reels

Voice as a Service (VAAS)

Freelancers and marketers are already selling:

• "Voiceovers for your YouTube video"

• "Narrate your blog in a podcast-style voice"

- "Convert your sales page into a high-converting audio clip"

Prices range from **$30 to $300+** depending on length, usage rights, and quality.

AI audio lets you speak with confidence—even if you never open your mouth.

◈ Reflection & Action: Chapter 30 – Monetizing AI Voice and Audio Tools

Reflect:

1. Do you enjoy written content, storytelling, or presenting—but don't like being on camera or recording your own voice?
2. Could you turn your writing or someone else's into an audio product, podcast, or voiceover service using AI?
3. What niche could you serve with AI audio—authors, YouTubers, educators, or business coaches?

Journal Prompt:
_"If I created an AI-powered voice product, it would be ________ and I would sell it to _______ who need help with ______."

Take Action:
◈ 1. Pick an AI Audio Tool to Experiment With
Try one from this list:

- **ElevenLabs** – For hyper-realistic narration
- **Descript** – For editing podcasts, videos, and scripts

- **Lovo.ai** or **Murf.ai** – For high-quality voiceovers
- **Play.ht** – For turning blog posts into audio instantly

◈ 2. Create a Short Audio Project
Options:

- Narrate a 3-minute blog post
- Record a sample ad voiceover
- Turn a chapter of your eBook into an audio file
- Voice a YouTube script with a professional AI voice

◈ 3. Offer It as a Service or Product
Post a gig on:

- **Fiverr**: "I'll turn your blog post into a narrated podcast"
- **Upwork**: "AI voiceovers for coaches, authors, and creators"
- **Gumroad**: Sell voice bundles, audio books, or voice packs
- **Email creators** offering to voice their content for free to start

◈ 4. Add It to Your Own Business

- Add AI voice narration to your sales pages or lead magnets
- Post "talking content" as reels or shorts
- Use it in audiobooks, training courses, or daily affirmations

Power Quote:

"In the future, your voice can be anywhere, all the time—and AI makes that future profitable."

— David Moore

Chapter 31: Generating Passive Income With AI Tools

Make It Once. Let AI Sell It Forever.

Passive income doesn't mean zero work—it means **front-loading effort for long-term payoff.** And with AI, that front-loading is faster, cheaper, and smarter than ever.

Whether you're creating digital products, building niche sites, or automating marketing, AI tools can help you set up **income streams that run while you sleep.**

This chapter walks you through the smartest ways to build, launch, and scale passive income assets using AI.

What Counts as Passive Income (AI Edition)?

Asset	How It Makes You Money
eBooks	Sell on Amazon, Gumroad, or bundles
Courses	Host on Teachable, Podia, or sell direct
Templates	Canva kits, Notion pages, prompt packs
Stock content	AI images, voiceovers, music, videos
Affiliate blogs	Monetized through product links
Digital downloads	Etsy, Payhip, Shopify
Newsletter referrals	Paid referral programs (Substack, Beehiiv)

AI helps you **create, publish, and promote** these assets 5x faster than doing it all manually.

Build Your First AI-Powered Passive Income Asset

1. Pick a Niche with Ongoing Demand

Look for:

- Parenting
- Fitness
- AI tools
- Spirituality
- Productivity
- Side hustles
- Self-publishing
- Etsy sellers

2. Ask AI to Generate the Content

Prompt:

"Create a 5,000-word eBook for beginner photographers on mastering smartphone shots. Include a table of contents and key takeaways per chapter."

Or:

"Write copy for a printable habit tracker, including title, benefits, and instructions."

3. Package It

Use:

- **Canva** for design
- **Notion** for templates
- **Google Docs** / **PDF** for downloadable guides

- **Gumroad / Payhip** to sell

4. Automate Your Marketing
Use AI for:

- Email welcome sequences
- Instagram captions and carousel posts
- Blog content for SEO
- Pinterest pin designs
- Landing page headlines and sales copy

5. Set It and Scale It
Once launched:

- Send traffic via ads or SEO
- Set up auto-responses for buyers
- Add upsells (e.g., workbook with ebook, or templates with course)

Example: $500/Month From a Single Digital Product

Let's say you:

- Use ChatGPT to write a 10-chapter eBook on "AI for Etsy Sellers"
- Design a matching workbook in Canva

- Bundle them together on Gumroad for $27
- Drive traffic via 3 weekly Instagram posts + 1 blog per week (all AI-written)

Sell 20 bundles/month = $540/month

In 3 months, your time investment pays itself off—then it's all profit.

Now, **imagine doing this 5 more times.**

AI Tools That Automate Passive Profit

Need	Tool
Writing content	ChatGPT, Jasper, Writesonic
Design + mockups	Canva, Kittl, Creative Fabrica
Stock visuals	Midjourney, DALL·E, Leonardo
Audio products	ElevenLabs, Descript
Templates + files	Notion, Google Docs, PDF builders
Selling platform	Gumroad, Payhip, Etsy
Email automation	ConvertKit, MailerLite, Beehiiv
Web pages	Carrd, Swipe Pages, Systeme.io

Passive income is no longer about waiting years.

With AI, you can **launch, test, and earn in weeks—not months.**

⟐ Reflection & Action: Chapter 31 – Generating Passive Income With AI Tools

Reflect:

1. What kind of digital product could you create once and sell

repeatedly—with help from AI?

2. Which skills or passions of yours could be turned into a low-cost, high-value asset?
3. What platform—Gumroad, Etsy, Amazon, or your own site—fits your audience and product best?

Journal Prompt:

_"If I launched one AI-powered passive income product this week, it would be _______ and I would sell it to _______ to help them _______."

Take Action:

◈ 1. Choose a Digital Product Format

Pick one to start with:

- eBook or short guide
- Canva template pack
- AI prompt bundle
- Printable habit tracker or planner
- Mini video/audio course
- Niche blog with affiliate links

◈ 2. Use AI to Generate the Core Content

Prompts:

"Write a 10-page eBook on time management for busy moms."

"Create 30 motivational affirmations for entrepreneurs to be turned into printable cards."

"Outline 10 Canva templates for small business Instagram pages."

◈ 3. Design and Package It

- Use **Canva** to design PDFs, templates, or mockups
- Export as high-quality downloadable files
- Upload to **Gumroad**, **Etsy**, or **Payhip**

◈ 4. Create AI-Powered Marketing Content

Prompt:

"Write an Instagram caption promoting a printable budget planner for students. Include 3 benefits and a call to action."

Repeat this for:

- Email sequence
- Blog post
- Pinterest pin text
- Product description

◈ 5. Automate and Track

- Set up automatic delivery emails
- Link to your product from bios, blogs, and ads
- Check sales weekly and tweak your strategy

Power Quote:

"With AI, you don't just earn while you sleep—you build while you dream."

— David Moore

Chapter 32: Selling AI-Enhanced Printables and Planners

Low-Cost to Make, High-Profit to Sell—Thanks to AI

Printables and planners are one of the **easiest, most profitable digital products** to launch. People buy them daily on Etsy, Gumroad, and Shopify—for everything from productivity and budgeting to fitness, mindset, and even self-care.

The best part? With AI, you can design them **faster**, **better**, and **with unique value** your competitors can't match.

Why Printables Sell Like Crazy

- Instant download = no shipping or inventory
- Evergreen appeal: budgeting, planning, self-improvement
- People love **organizing, tracking, and journaling**
- Easy to personalize or niche down
- AI helps generate content, layout ideas, and even keywords

Printables are the **perfect entry point** for turning creativity into income.

Popular Printable & Planner Niches

Category	Examples
Productivity	Daily planners, to-do lists, time-blocking sheets
Finance	Budget trackers, debt payoff charts, savings challenges
Wellness	Meal plans, workout logs, mental health journals
Business	Social media calendars, content planners, Etsy shop checklists
Education	Homeschool worksheets, study guides, test prep
Spirituality	Moon trackers, gratitude journals, tarot spreads
Kids & Family	Chore charts, reward coupons, birthday party packs

How AI Enhances Every Step

1. Brainstorm Ideas

Prompt:

"List 25 printable planner ideas for moms who run side hustles."

2. Write the Content

Prompt:

"Write a 4-week productivity planner with weekly themes, daily prompts, and motivational quotes."

3. Generate Visual Elements

- Use **DALL·E** or **Midjourney** to create:
  - Watercolor-style icons
  - Vision board backgrounds
  - Themed page illustrations

4. Design in Canva or Kittl

- Plug in AI-written copy
- Use drag-and-drop templates
- Export as high-res PDFs

5. Create Multiple Versions

- Color vs. black & white
- Letter size vs. A4
- Editable vs. print-only
- Bundle multiple files for higher pricing

Platforms to Sell Your Printables

Platform	Best For
Etsy	High-volume traffic, great for printables
Gumroad	Simple setup, good for niche or social selling
Payhip	Flexible pricing, affiliate support
Shopify + Digital Downloads	Scale your own store
Creative Market	Higher-end templates + bundles

Pricing and Upselling Ideas

- Single page: $2–$5
- Planner bundle (20+ pages): $12–$27

- Seasonal or themed bundles: $17–$47
- Upsell: Add a Trello board, Notion version, or matching phone wallpapers

Example: From Prompt to Profit

1. Prompt:

"Create a 30-day gratitude journal with daily prompts, quotes, and reflection spaces."

1. Output:
   Use ChatGPT for content → Canva for layout → Midjourney for cover art
2. Package:
   Sell as a printable bundle + a mobile-friendly version
3. Market:
   Post preview pages on Pinterest and Instagram using AI captions

Sell 25 copies/month at $15 = $375/month

AI turns a simple idea into a professional, sellable product—in a single afternoon.

◈ Reflection & Action: Chapter 32 – Selling AI-Enhanced Printables and Planners

Reflect:

1. What type of printable would you love to create—planners, journals, trackers, or educational worksheets?
2. Who would your ideal customer be—busy moms, small business owners, students, teachers, or creatives?
3. Could you use AI to generate prompts, layouts, quotes, or imagery to speed up the process?

Journal Prompt:

_"If I created a printable planner this week, it would help _______ stay on track with _______ and I'd sell it on _______ for ______."

Take Action:

◈ 1. Choose a Niche + Product Idea

Prompt example:

"Give me 10 printable planner ideas for beginner entrepreneurs working from home."

Pick one and move to step 2.

◈ 2. Use ChatGPT to Write the Content

Examples:

- "Generate a 4-week self-care tracker with daily reflection prompts."
- "Create 30 positive affirmations to include in a printable gratitude journal."

◈ 3. Design With Canva or Kittl

- Use pre-made templates or start from scratch
- Insert your AI-generated content
- Export as PDF (Letter, A4, and mobile sizes)

◈ 4. Upload and Sell

Choose a platform:

- **Etsy** for wide exposure
- **Gumroad** for social and niche sales
- **Payhip** for affiliate-friendly digital stores

◈ 5. Promote With AI Help

Prompt:

"Write an Instagram caption promoting a printable daily productivity planner for moms. Include 3 benefits and a call to action."

Also create:

- Pinterest pins
- TikTok video scripts
- Email newsletters

Power Quote:

"AI gives you the power to turn thoughts into templates—and ideas into income."

— David Moore

Chapter 33: Offering AI Automation Services to Small Businesses

Help Businesses Save Time—and They'll Pay You Every Month

Every day, small business owners juggle emails, invoices, scheduling, social media, customer follow-ups, and more. Most of them **don't know AI can automate 50–80% of that work**—but you do.

By offering AI-powered automation services, you can become the person who helps businesses save time, cut costs, and scale faster. And because these tools run behind the scenes, this becomes a **high-retention, recurring-income business** for you.

Why AI Automation Is a Goldmine

- Business owners want *results*, not tech headaches
- Most don't know these tools exist (or how to use them)
- Once automation is set up, it runs forever
- You can charge monthly fees for upkeep and updates
- You don't need to code—just know the right tools + use cases

Types of Tasks You Can Automate

Category	Automation Example
Email	Auto-reply to inquiries, send follow-ups, trigger drip sequences
Scheduling	Auto-book calls from form entries, send reminders via SMS or email
CRM	Add new leads to a list, tag based on preferences, trigger nurture workflows
E-commerce	Thank-you emails, abandoned cart follow-ups, review requests
Social media	Auto-generate captions, repurpose content, schedule posts
Payments	Auto-invoice clients, send receipts, track recurring payments
Internal ops	Send Slack alerts, update spreadsheets, generate reports

Tools You'll Want in Your Automation Toolkit

Tool	What It Does
Zapier	Connects apps and automates workflows across platforms
Make (Integromat)	Visual automation builder—great for complex flows
Pabbly	Budget-friendly Zapier alternative
OpenAI / ChatGPT API	Automate writing, data processing, analysis
Airtable / Notion	Smart databases that automate content or client management
Calendly	Schedule automation for coaches, consultants, service pros
MailerLite / ConvertKit	Auto-send newsletters, tag leads, trigger sequences

Real-World Business Automation Examples

Local Gym

- Auto-add new signups from website form into MailerLite
- Send welcome email sequence with class schedule
- Auto-send birthday discounts via SMS

Online Coach

- Create onboarding flow with Notion + Calendly
- Auto-generate course access email after payment

- Weekly AI-written newsletter sent via ConvertKit

E-commerce Brand

- Recover abandoned carts with follow-up emails
- Auto-request reviews after 14 days
- Auto-tag VIP buyers and offer loyalty bonuses

How to Package and Sell Automation Services

Offer	What You Do	Price Range
Audit + Strategy	Identify automation opportunities	$100–$300
One-time setup	Build custom workflows	$500–$2,000
Monthly support	Maintain and optimize	$100–$500/ month
DIY templates	Sell pre-made automation flows	$27–$197

Who to Pitch First

Start with:

- Coaches and consultants
- Real estate agents
- Fitness studios
- Online shops

- Wedding vendors
- Freelancers and service providers

They're busy. They'll pay to get their time back.

Automation is no longer just for big companies.

It's now a small business superpower—delivered by people like you.

◈ Reflection & Action: Chapter 33 – Offering AI Automation Services to Small Businesses

Reflect:

1. Which types of businesses do you already know or interact with—fitness coaches, Etsy sellers, salon owners, consultants?
2. What repetitive tasks could you help them automate using AI tools?
3. Could you see yourself offering this as a monthly service, or packaging templates for DIY users?

Journal Prompt:

_"If I offered AI automation services, I'd focus on helping ________ automate ________ using tools like ______."

Take Action:

◈ 1. Choose a Business Type to Help First

Pick a niche you understand or can easily research—like personal trainers, online creators, or real estate agents.

◈ 2. Run an Automation Audit (with AI's Help)

Prompt:

"List 10 common business tasks that an online coach does daily or weekly, and suggest how they can be automated with tools like Zapier, Calendly, or MailerLite."

◈ **3. Build One Working Automation Flow**

Start simple:

- New form submission → Auto-tag in ConvertKit → Send welcome email
- New order on Shopify → Send thank-you email + request review in 10 days
- Booked Calendly session → Add to CRM + trigger follow-up email sequence

◈ **4. Create a Demo Video or Template to Showcase**

- Use **Loom** or **Descript** to record a walkthrough
- Share in Facebook groups, Reddit threads, or LinkedIn posts
- Offer a free audit to 3 businesses in exchange for testimonials

◈ **5. Package Your Offer**

Examples:

- "Done-for-you automation setup for coaches – $497 one-time"
- "Monthly automation support for your digital business – $197/month"
- "Zapier workflows for Etsy sellers – $97 DIY kit"

Power Quote:

"Businesses don't pay for bots. They pay for time, sanity, and scale—and AI automation delivers all three."

— David Moore

Chapter 34: Creating AI-Driven Content for YouTube Channels

No Camera? No Problem. Let AI Be Your Co-Creator.

YouTube is one of the most profitable platforms in the creator economy—and with AI, you can build a channel **without showing your face, recording your voice, or editing for hours**.

From scriptwriting to voiceover to video editing, AI tools can help you create **engaging, monetizable videos at scale**, perfect for niche content, tutorials, top 10 lists, or even animated storytelling.

Why YouTube Is Still the King

- Billions of users = huge reach
- Passive income from AdSense, sponsorships, and affiliate links
- High-ranking YouTube videos also show up in Google Search
- You can build a brand—or just earn from niche faceless content
- AI cuts your content creation time by 80%

Types of AI-Powered YouTube Channels You Can Start

Channel Type	AI Use Case
Top 10 / List videos	ChatGPT for scripts, ElevenLabs for voiceover, Pictory for video
Motivational / Quotes	AI for voice, visuals, and background music
Educational Explainers	ChatGPT for research, Canva + AI video tools for visuals
Faceless News / Recaps	Daily trending scripts + AI narration
Product Reviews	AI-generated video + affiliate links
History / Mystery / True Crime	Storytelling + atmospheric AI music and visuals
AI Experiments Channel	Showcase cool AI outputs, tools, and automation

AI Tools to Build Your Channel

Need	Tool
Scriptwriting	ChatGPT, Jasper
Voiceovers	ElevenLabs, Murf, Lovo
Stock video	Pexels, Pixabay, Storyblocks
Video creation	Pictory, InVideo, Runway, Animoto
Editing	Descript, CapCut, Canva Pro
Thumbnail design	Canva, Kittl
Music / FX	Uppbeat, Epidemic Sound, Soundraw

The AI YouTube Workflow

Step 1: Pick a Niche + Video Topic

Prompt:

"Give me 20 YouTube video ideas for a channel about side hustles."

Then pick one and move to step 2.

Step 2: Write the Script

Prompt:

"Write a 500-word script for a YouTube video titled '5 AI Tools That Can Make You Money in 2025' with an engaging intro and CTA."

Step 3: Create the Voiceover

Use ElevenLabs or Murf to generate natural-sounding narration in your chosen tone.

Step 4: Add Visuals

- Use Pictory to match visuals to your script
- OR grab stock video clips from Pexels and combine in Canva or CapCut
- Add captions or motion elements using Descript or Animoto

Step 5: Upload, Optimize, Promote

- Create an eye-catching thumbnail in Canva
- Use AI to write your video title, description, and tags
- Promote your video via Instagram Reels, TikToks, or newsletters

Monetization Options

Method	When It Pays
YouTube AdSense	After 1,000 subs + 4,000 watch hours
Affiliate links	Right away (ex: AI tool links in video descriptions)
Sponsored content	Once you have an audience or niche authority
Digital product plug	Link to your eBook, course, or templates
Newsletter opt-ins	Grow your list from day one

Sample Channel Strategy: 1 Video/Week

Niche: AI for small business
Plan:

- Script + voice with ChatGPT + ElevenLabs
- Visuals with Pictory
- Thumbnails in Canva
- Promote on Twitter and Pinterest
- Include affiliate links in every description

In 90 days, with 12–15 quality videos, you could start earning on autopilot.

The future of content creation isn't about being on camera—
it's about being consistent, valuable, and automated.

◈ Reflection & Action: Chapter 34 – Creating AI-Driven Content for YouTube Channels

Reflect:

1. What kind of YouTube channel could you realistically run without ever showing your face?
2. Do you have a niche or topic you enjoy—like tech, self-help, motivation, money, or storytelling?
3. How could you use AI tools to make the process smoother and more consistent?

Journal Prompt:

_"If I launched a faceless YouTube channel this month, it would focus on _______ and my first 3 video topics would be ______."

Take Action:

◈ **1. Pick a Channel Niche + Starter Topics**

Prompt:

"Give me 10 YouTube video topics for a faceless channel about AI tools and side hustles."

◈ **2. Generate a Script With AI**

Prompt:

"Write a 600-word YouTube script titled 'Top 5 Passive Income Tools Powered by AI' with a hook, tips, and call to action."

◈ **3. Create Voiceover Using AI**

- Use **ElevenLabs**, **Murf**, or **Lovo.ai**
- Select a voice that fits your channel's tone
- Export as MP3

◈ **4. Build Your Video**

Use:

- **Pictory** to match visuals to narration
- OR edit clips manually using **Canva Pro**, **Descript**, or **CapCut**

◈ 5. Upload + Optimize With AI

Prompt:

"Write a catchy YouTube title, 2-sentence description, and 10 relevant hashtags for a video about passive income AI tools."

◈ 6. Monetize Early With Affiliate Links

- Add links in the description for tools mentioned
- Mention a freebie to build an email list
- Add a CTA to download your guide, planner, or product

Power Quote:

"The future isn't faceless—it's frictionless. With AI, anyone can be a YouTube creator."

— David Moore

Chapter 35: Building and Selling AI-Powered Digital Templates

Sell Solutions Instead of Services

Templates are one of the smartest digital assets you can sell. Why? Because people don't want to build from scratch—they want a **shortcut to success.**

And with AI, you can create beautiful, functional, and profitable templates in less time than ever. From Canva graphics to Notion dashboards, AI prompt bundles to email funnels, **you can package your expertise once and sell it thousands of times.**

Why Templates Are a Goldmine

- Fast to create and launch
- High perceived value
- Endless niches (biz, health, self-care, tech, education)
- Easy to bundle or upsell
- Sell on multiple platforms (Gumroad, Etsy, your site)
- Customers love them—and come back for more

Top-Selling Digital Template Categories

Category	Examples
Productivity	Notion dashboards, to-do lists, habit trackers
Business	Client onboarding kits, content calendars, SOP templates
Social Media	Canva post templates, caption bundles, story highlights
Finance	Budget spreadsheets, income trackers, savings planners
Wellness	Self-care planners, journal templates, gratitude prompts
Education	Lesson plans, study guides, quiz templates
AI Prompt Packs	ChatGPT workflows for bloggers, marketers, creators

AI-Enhanced Template Ideas

1. ChatGPT Prompt Libraries

Create niche prompt packs for:

- Real estate agents
- Etsy sellers
- Life coaches
- YouTubers
- Course creators

2. Canva Template Packs

Use AI to:

- Write copy for Instagram carousels
- Generate motivational quotes
- Suggest post themes

3. Notion / Airtable Templates
Let AI help:

- Structure databases
- Pre-fill with formulas or prompts
- Automate task and goal trackers

4. Funnel or Email Templates
Use ChatGPT to generate:

- Lead magnet copy
- Email sequences
- Landing page outlines
- Upsell flows

Create Once, Sell Forever: The Workflow

Step 1: Pick a Niche & Template Type

Prompt:

"Give me 15 digital template ideas for side hustle moms who sell on Etsy."

Step 2: Build With AI Support

Use ChatGPT to:

- Generate placeholder content
- Add instructional copy
- Include examples and bonus tips

Step 3: Design & Format

- Canva or Kittl for visuals
- Google Docs, Notion, or Airtable for planners or dashboards
- Convert to downloadable PDFs, editable links, or zip files

Step 4: Create Product Mockups
Use Canva or Smartmockups to present your product professionally.

Step 5: List It for Sale

- Gumroad
- Etsy (for PDF templates)
- Your own site
- Ko-fi, Payhip, or Creative Market

Bonus Tip: Bundle and Upsell

- Starter pack → Premium pack
- Single template → Niche bundle

- Add tutorial video, quick-start guide, or AI bonus prompts

Example:

$19 – Basic planner

$39 – Pro version with bonus Notion dashboard

$97 – "Ultimate Business Bundle" with 7 tools and private video walkthrough

Templates are more than downloads—they're **done-for-you wins** people will gladly pay for.

◈ Reflection & Action: Chapter 35 – Building and Selling AI-Powered Digital Templates

Reflect:

1. What type of templates have you personally used—or wished you had?
2. Who could benefit from a shortcut you've figured out—Etsy sellers, coaches, content creators, students?
3. How could you use AI to create content, structure, or design these templates faster?

Journal Prompt:

_"If I launched a digital template today, it would help ________ achieve ________ without having to ______."

Take Action:

◈ 1. Pick a Niche + Template Type

Prompt:

"Suggest 10 digital templates I could sell to first-time entrepreneurs trying to grow on Instagram."

Choose one and move to step 2.

◈ **2. Use AI to Draft the Content**

Prompts:

- "Create a 30-day Instagram caption calendar for fitness coaches."
- "Write 10 onboarding email templates for virtual assistants."
- "Outline a Notion dashboard to help freelancers manage clients, tasks, and payments."

◈ **3. Design the Product**

Use:

- **Canva** for social or planner templates
- **Notion, Airtable**, or **Google Sheets** for dashboards and trackers
- Add helpful AI-generated copy, placeholders, or tips

◈ **4. Package and Mock It Up**

- Save as editable links, PDFs, or .zip files
- Create product mockups using **Canva** or **Smartmockups**
- Write a simple sales page using ChatGPT

◈ **5. Publish and Promote**

- Upload to **Etsy**, **Gumroad**, or **Payhip**

- Share in niche Facebook groups, Reddit subs, or TikTok videos

- Create an email opt-in or upsell funnel using the same AI tools

Power Quote:

"Templates don't just save time—they sell trust. AI helps you deliver both at scale."

— David Moore

Chapter 36: Using AI to Create & Sell Niche Newsletters

Build a Loyal Audience. Monetize With Every Send.

Newsletters are back—and smarter than ever. What used to take hours of research and writing, you can now create in minutes using AI.

Whether you want to build an audience, earn through affiliate links, or even get **paid per subscriber**, newsletters are a powerful long-term business model. And AI gives you the edge to **stay consistent, stay valuable, and stay profitable.**

Why Newsletters Work (Even in 2025)

- You own your audience (unlike social media)
- Email is still the highest-ROI channel for marketers
- Platforms like Substack and Beehiiv pay you to grow
- You can monetize with affiliates, ads, courses, and more
- AI tools make creating high-quality content ridiculously easy

Newsletter Niches That Are Thriving

Niche	Example Focus
AI Tools	"5 AI Hacks for Marketers"
Investing	"Crypto Moves This Week"
Wellness	"The Daily Calm: Mental Health Tips"
Side Hustles	"$500/Week From Home Ideas"
Relationships	"Smart Dating Tips for Professionals"
Pop Culture	"What Everyone's Talking About This Week"
Creator Economy	"Tools, Trends & Tips for Creators"

How to Use AI to Write Great Newsletters

1. Curate the Best Info

Prompt:

"Summarize 3 trending stories about AI business tools in less than 150 words each."

2. Write in a Relatable Tone

Prompt:

"Rewrite this summary in a fun, conversational voice with a call to action."

3. Add Visuals and Headlines

- Use Canva or Unsplash for free images
- Ask ChatGPT for punchy subject lines, headlines, and CTAs
- Include emojis, formatting, and personal stories for connection

4. Schedule and Send

Use tools like:

- **Beehiiv** (great for monetization + referrals)
- **ConvertKit** (automation + creator-friendly)
- **Substack** (easy for discovery + subscriptions)
- **MailerLite** or **Flodesk** (clean design, affordable)

Monetization Options

Method	When to Use
Affiliate links	Add product links with your tracking code
Sponsored spots	Sell ad space to brands in your niche
Premium tiers	Charge for weekly deep dives or bonus content
Courses / ebooks	Promote your own products to your audience
Referral rewards	Platforms like Beehiiv pay per referred subscriber
Freelance ghostwriting	Write newsletters for other creators or businesses

Sample Strategy: "The Weekend AI Hustle" Newsletter

- Every Saturday: 3 tools, 1 case study, 1 prompt
- Written in a casual, practical tone
- Monetized via affiliate links for AI tools
- Linked to an eBook: "100 AI Side Hustle Prompts"
- Cross-promoted via Twitter, Instagram, and LinkedIn

You don't need to be a guru—just someone who curates, simplifies, and shows up.

With AI, you can **create a newsletter people love—and one that pays you back.**

◈ Reflection & Action: Chapter 36 – Using AI to Create & Sell Niche Newsletters

Reflect:

1. What kind of email content would you love to create—or read—each week?
2. Who could benefit from curated, helpful, or entertaining info you send consistently?
3. How could you use AI to generate content faster, stay consistent, and grow?

Journal Prompt:

"If I started a weekly newsletter, it would be called ________ and every issue would help readers ________ in 5 minutes or less."

Take Action:

◈ 1. Choose Your Niche and Format

Prompt:

"List 10 creative newsletter ideas for someone who loves AI, productivity, and making money online."

◈ 2. Use AI to Draft Your First Issue

Prompt:

"Write a 3-section newsletter for side hustlers including one trending tool, one tip, and one weekly challenge. Keep it casual and fun."

◈ 3. Choose a Platform
Options:

- **Substack** – easy discovery and subscriptions
- **Beehiiv** – powerful growth tools and referrals
- **ConvertKit** – great for creators with products
- **MailerLite** – budget-friendly with automation

◈ 4. Launch With a Freebie or Hook
Ideas:

- "Subscribe to get the free guide: 50 AI Side Hustle Prompts"
- "Join 1,000+ creators getting weekly growth hacks"
- "Every Friday: 3 tools, 1 tactic, and no fluff."

◈ 5. Promote + Monetize
Use ChatGPT to:

- Write social posts promoting your newsletter
- Craft affiliate blurbs or product plugs
- Create referral or welcome email flows

Power Quote:
"You don't need a massive audience to make money—just a helpful voice in one inbox at a time."
— David Moore

Chapter 37: Licensing AI Creations for Royalties and Residuals

Create It Once. Get Paid Again and Again.

One of the most overlooked—but most powerful—ways to make money with AI is through **licensing**. Whether it's images, music, voiceovers, code snippets, or written content, you can license what you create with AI and **collect royalties, usage fees, or platform payouts** again and again.

Licensing isn't just about art—it's about **intellectual property**. And with AI, you now have the ability to create high-quality, licensable assets fast.

What You Can License with AI

Type of Content	Examples
AI Art / Illustrations	Midjourney or DALL·E creations sold on stock sites
AI Music / Beats	Soundraw or Amper tracks licensed to creators
Voiceovers	ElevenLabs-generated audio sold for podcasts, ads, or videos
Written Content	ChatGPT-created articles, email packs, or product descriptions
Templates / Prompts	Prompt packs for specific industries sold with usage rights
Code / Automations	Zapier workflows, GPT scripts, AI chatbots

Platforms to Sell or License AI Creations

Platform	Best For
Creative Fabrica	Printables, graphics, AI art
Artlist / Pond5 / AudioJungle	Royalty-free music and voiceovers
Storyblocks / Envato Elements	Visual assets and video elements
PromptBase	Sell prompt templates and AI prompt packs
Ko-fi / Gumroad	License directly with usage rights
Fiverr Pro	Custom license deals with commercial clients
Etsy (Commercial Use)	Offer extended license add-ons for digital files

How to License Your Work Effectively

1. Clarify Usage Rights

You can sell:

- **Personal Use Only** – For individuals (non-commercial)
- **Commercial Use** – For business, resale, client work
- **Exclusive Use** – Higher price, one buyer only
- **Extended License** – Mass use, ads, product creation

Always specify what your buyers can and can't do. Use clear license terms.

2. Use AI to Help Create License Docs

Prompt:

"Write a short license agreement for a Canva template sold for commercial use."

3. Build Collections, Not Just One-Offs

Bundle multiple assets:

- 100 AI-generated textures
- 50 royalty-free beats
- 25 voiceover samples in different tones
- 10 Notion dashboards with business use rights

4. Offer Custom Licensing Tiers

- Basic: $15 (personal use)
- Pro: $45 (commercial use)
- Agency: $99+ (mass redistribution)

Use Gumroad or Ko-fi to structure pricing.

Real-World Example: Licensing AI Beats

- Use **Soundraw**, **Amper**, or **AIVA** to generate royalty-free music
- Export 10–20 variations in different moods
- Upload to **Pond5**, **Artlist**, or sell directly via **Gumroad**
- Add clear license terms: royalty-free use for YouTube, ads, or games

- Charge $25–$99 per track + upsell bundles

Licensing means **you don't trade time for money—you trade assets for royalties.**

And with AI, you can build an entire portfolio in weeks, not years.

◈ Reflection & Action: Chapter 37 – Licensing AI Creations for Royalties and Residuals

Reflect:

1. What kind of AI creations are you naturally drawn to—art, music, writing, voiceovers, prompts, or code?
2. Could you build a small, focused library of high-quality assets that others would pay to use?
3. How could you protect your work while giving others value through fair licensing?

Journal Prompt:

_"If I created an AI-powered asset library, it would focus on _______ and be used by ________ for ______."

Take Action:

◈ **1. Choose an Asset Type to License**

Prompt:

"List 10 creative digital assets I can generate using AI that are suitable for licensing to content creators."

◈ **2. Create and Curate With AI Tools**

Examples:

- **Midjourney**: "Generate 25 vintage-style watercolor backgrounds."

- **ChatGPT**: "Write 100 micro-email subject lines for coaches."

- **ElevenLabs**: "Record 10 voiceovers in different tones for YouTube intros."

- **Soundraw**: "Produce upbeat instrumental tracks for lifestyle vloggers."

◈ 3. Package With Clear Licensing Terms

Prompt:

"Create a short, easy-to-understand license for commercial use of a digital planner template."

◈ 4. List Your Products on Licensing Platforms

- **Creative Fabrica**, **Etsy**, or **Gumroad** for printables, art, and prompts

- **AudioJungle**, **Artlist**, or **Pond5** for music and voiceovers

- Use bundles or multi-tiered pricing for broader appeal

◈ 5. Promote and Protect

- Use watermarking or demo previews for previews

- Include license text in every download

- Promote your asset store on social media, newsletters, or niche marketplaces

Power Quote:

"With AI, every asset you create becomes a potential royalty stream. Own your output, license your genius."

— David Moore

Chapter 38: Using AI to Build and Sell Online Courses

Teach What You Know—Faster and Smarter With AI

You don't need to be a "guru" to sell an online course. You just need to help someone solve a specific problem. Whether it's learning Canva, launching a side hustle, or automating tasks with ChatGPT—**people will pay for clear, guided instruction.**

And thanks to AI, building a course no longer takes months. You can script, structure, design, and even market a complete course using tools that accelerate your creativity.

Why Courses Are Evergreen Income Machines

- One-time creation → lifelong sales
- Highly scalable, high-profit margins
- Builds your brand and authority
- You can teach with slides, screen shares, audio, or faceless videos
- AI makes the content creation process 3× faster

Best Niches for AI-Assisted Courses

Niche	Course Ideas
AI & Tech	"How to Make Passive Income with ChatGPT"
Business	"Start a Freelance Service with Zero Clients"
Productivity	"Mastering Notion in 7 Days"
Side Hustles	"Build and Launch a Digital Product in a Weekend"
Wellness	"The Mental Reset: 10-Day Guided Self-Care Program"
Marketing	"Instagram Growth Strategies for Solopreneurs"
Creators	"Faceless YouTube Channel Bootcamp"

How AI Builds Your Course With You

1. Outline Your Curriculum

Prompt:

"Create a 6-module course outline on starting a print-on-demand side hustle with no upfront cost."

2. Write the Lessons and Scripts

Prompt:

"Write the script for Module 1, Lesson 1: 'Introduction to POD and Marketplace Platforms.' Keep it beginner-friendly and engaging."

3. Create Slides, PDFs, and Downloads

- Use **Canva, Kittl**, or **Tome.app**
- Ask ChatGPT to create key points, exercises, summaries, and checklists
- Include AI-generated visuals or infographics

4. Record the Content

- Use screen recorders like **Loom, OBS Studio**, or **Tella**

- Use **ElevenLabs** for AI narration (if going faceless)
- Add subtitles using **Descript** or **CapCut**

5. Upload and Sell
Best platforms:

- **Gumroad** – easy to start, low fees
- **Teachable** – great for multi-course libraries
- **Podia** – built-in email + sales pages
- **Thinkific, Kajabi, Thrivecart Learn** – for pros scaling up

Monetization Options

Model	What You Do
One-time course	Charge $27–$297 per course
Bundles	Sell multiple mini-courses together
Membership	Monthly fee for ongoing content
Coaching upgrade	Add 1:1 sessions or group support
Upsells	eBooks, templates, private communities

Example Strategy: 1-Day AI Mini Course

- Title: "Make $100/Week With AI-Generated Printables"
- 5 video lessons (5–10 mins each)
- Includes: scripts, prompts, Canva templates

- Price: $47
- Promote via Instagram, newsletter, and TikTok

Build it once. Sell it forever.

The best teachers aren't always the loudest—they're the most helpful.

AI gives you the tools to teach, reach, and earn—on your own terms.

◈ Reflection & Action: Chapter 38 – Using AI to Build and Sell Online Courses

Reflect:

1. What topic have people asked you for help with—or something you've figured out the hard way?
2. Could you break that topic into steps and teach it with slides, screen recordings, or even just audio?
3. How can you use AI to save time scripting, designing, and promoting your course?

Journal Prompt:

_"If I launched a mini-course this month, it would teach ________ in ________ days and help people go from ________ to ______."

Take Action:

◈ 1. Choose a Topic You Can Teach Simply

Prompt:

"List 10 online course ideas I can create in under a week using AI tools, based on side hustles and productivity."

◈ 2. Use AI to Build the Curriculum

Prompt:

"Create a 6-module outline for a beginner-friendly course on making passive income with AI tools like ChatGPT and Canva."

◈ **3. Script the Lessons With AI Help**

Prompt:

"Write the script for Module 1: Getting Started With AI Side Hustles. Keep it clear, conversational, and practical."

◈ **4. Design Materials and Record**

- Use **Canva** to create slide decks
- Record with **Loom**, **OBS**, or **Tella**
- Use **ElevenLabs** or **Murf** for faceless narration
- Add handouts, checklists, or bonus prompts created by ChatGPT

◈ **5. Upload and Sell**

- Use **Gumroad**, **Podia**, or **Teachable**
- Write a landing page with ChatGPT
- Set your price and create a simple upsell funnel

◈ **6. Promote Your Course With AI**

Prompt:

"Write a launch email, Instagram caption, and TikTok script to promote my new mini-course on passive income with AI tools."

Power Quote:

"If you've solved a problem once, you can teach it forever—and AI makes that process faster, smarter, and scalable."

— David Moore

Chapter 39: Combining Multiple AI Income Streams Into One Digital Empire

The Real Power Play? Synergy.

Making money with AI doesn't have to be about **just one stream of income**. The smartest creators and entrepreneurs don't stop at printables, or newsletters, or automation—they **stack their skills** and turn them into a full ecosystem.

This is where the magic happens: your newsletter promotes your YouTube channel, which feeds into your template store, which upsells into your course... and every piece is powered by AI.

Why You Should Build an AI-Powered Ecosystem

- Diversifies your revenue
- Increases customer lifetime value
- Automates content creation and promotion
- Builds brand authority and trust
- Creates a "money flywheel" that compounds over time

Example: The Digital Empire Blueprint

Niche: Helping solopreneurs make money online using AI

Asset	Purpose	AI Tools
Newsletter	Build trust + list	ChatGPT + Beehiiv
YouTube Channel	Traffic + affiliate	ElevenLabs + Pictory
Printables Store	Low-ticket income	Canva + ChatGPT
AI Prompt Pack	Mid-ticket offer	PromptLayer + Gumroad
Online Course	High-ticket income	ChatGPT + Loom + Canva
Automation Services	Custom freelance work	Zapier + Make + GPT-4
Community	Loyalty + referrals	Circle or Skool
Ebook / Guide	Lead magnet or tripwire	ChatGPT + Vellum

Each piece supports the others. One sale leads to another. One post fuels multiple platforms.

How to Stack It, Step-by-Step

Step 1: Pick a Clear Niche + Mission

Prompt:

"Help me define a personal brand that helps content creators use AI to grow faster and smarter."

Step 2: Start With a Simple Offer

Example:

- $27 eBook: "100 ChatGPT Prompts to Grow Your Brand"
- Free newsletter with weekly tips + affiliate links

Step 3: Add One Channel at a Time

- YouTube → Promote your prompt pack

- Gumroad → Offer your ebook
- Beehiiv → Collect emails, promote your video
- Canva shop → Link from newsletter and course

Step 4: Automate with AI Tools

- Use ChatGPT to repurpose content
- Use Zapier to connect sales to email flows
- Use Pictory to turn articles into YouTube videos
- Use ElevenLabs to narrate social posts or YouTube shorts

Sample AI Empire Funnel

1. **Instagram Reel** (script by ChatGPT)
2. Leads to **Newsletter Signup** (via Beehiiv)
3. Auto-sends **Welcome Sequence** + Freebie
4. Sells **Prompt Pack** ($19) → Upsell to Mini Course ($49)
5. **Course** leads to Community Invite ($12/mo)
6. Community members upgrade to **Coaching or Services**

You don't need to build it all at once.

But the real money comes when your ideas, content, and offers work **together**—powered by AI behind the scenes.

◈ Reflection & Action: Chapter 39 – Combining Multiple AI Income Streams Into One Digital Empire

Reflect:

1. Which of your AI-powered projects could naturally connect—like a YouTube channel promoting your templates or a newsletter that feeds into your course?
2. What's your zone of genius—and how can you build around it with multiple offers?
3. What part of your current system can AI automate to save you time or scale faster?

Journal Prompt:
_"My digital ecosystem would start with ________ and connect to ________ so that every piece helps grow ______."

Take Action:

◈ 1. Map Out Your Empire Vision

Prompt:
"Help me outline a digital ecosystem that starts with an AI newsletter and expands into a course, template store, and YouTube channel."

◈ 2. Pick 2 Complementary Offers to Launch Together

Examples:

- AI Prompt Pack + Email Newsletter
- Mini Course + Canva Template Bundle
- Ebook + Private Community Access

◈ 3. Use AI to Connect the Dots

Prompts:

- "Write a welcome email that links to my YouTube channel and course."

- "Create a CTA to include in my video that promotes my prompt pack."

- "Write a 3-email funnel to upsell buyers of my ebook into a mini-course."

◈ 4. Automate Your Funnel

- Use **Zapier** or **Make** to sync sales → email → access

- Use **ChatGPT** to repurpose content across platforms

- Use **Canva**, **Pictory**, or **ElevenLabs** to multiply your output

◈ 5. Track and Optimize

- Look at which offer gets the most engagement

- Use AI to analyze feedback and revise content

- Expand with upsells, affiliate deals, or new bundles

Power Quote:

"An empire isn't built in a day—but with AI, it can be built in less time, with more leverage, and endless potential."

— David Moore

Chapter 40: Your AI Money Blueprint – Final Steps & Next Moves

You Now Hold the Map. The Next Move Is Yours.

You've made it to the end—but really, this is the beginning. You've explored over three dozen ways to use AI to earn income, build assets, and create a future on your terms.

From printables to prompt packs, newsletters to niche channels, coaching to courses—you've now seen how **AI doesn't replace you—it multiplies your ability to create, connect, and cash in.**

Now it's time to focus, take action, and build something you're proud of.

Your AI Money Blueprint Checklist

◈ Pick your **core niche** (what problem do you help solve?)
◈ Choose your **starter stream** (printables, prompts, video, etc.)
◈ Use AI to build your **first product or service**
◈ Set up your **sales platform** (Gumroad, Beehiiv, Etsy, etc.)
◈ Automate your **marketing and delivery**
◈ Add a **second offer** (ebook, template, mini course)
◈ Create content that **feeds the system** (YouTube, IG, newsletter)
◈ Track what's working—and keep stacking wins

What To Do in the Next 7 Days

Day 1–2: Choose a niche and a single monetizable idea
Day 3–4: Use AI to create your first product or offer
Day 5: Build a landing page or storefront
Day 6: Promote using AI-written emails or posts

Day 7: Launch + gather feedback
Then refine. Iterate. Scale.

What To Avoid

◈ Don't try to build 10 income streams at once
◈ Don't obsess over perfection—start, then polish
◈ Don't assume you need followers to earn (you don't)
◈ Don't stop just because something flops—pivot instead
◈ Don't hoard your ideas—share them, test them, sell them

What To Double Down On

◈ Consistency beats complexity
◈ One strong offer can fund your freedom
◈ Repurpose content across multiple platforms
◈ Talk to your audience—then solve their problems
◈ Let AI do the heavy lifting so you can focus on vision

The Real Secret? Start Messy. Learn Loud. Grow Relentlessly.

Most people wait. Wait until they feel ready. Until the brand is perfect. Until someone gives them permission.

But you're not most people.

You now understand how AI can help you create, earn, and thrive—**not someday, but now.**

The next move is yours. Make it count.

⟐ Reflection & Action: Chapter 40 – Your AI Money Blueprint – Final Steps & Next Moves

Reflect:

1. What single AI-powered project are you most excited to start right now?
2. How will you commit to taking daily, imperfect action rather than waiting for "perfect"?
3. Who can you share your journey with—an accountability partner, mentor, or community?

Journal Prompt:

_"My first step toward building my AI-powered income this week is _______. I will track my progress by _______ and celebrate wins by _______."

Take Action:

⟐ **1. Choose Your Starter Project**

Pick one income stream from this book that excites you the most.

⟐ **2. Set a 7-Day Action Plan**

Map out daily tasks to build, launch, and promote your first offer.

⟐ **3. Share Your Goal Publicly**

Post on social media, tell a friend, or join an AI creator group for support.

⟐ **4. Use AI Tools Daily**

Leverage ChatGPT, Canva, Midjourney, ElevenLabs, or others to speed progress.

⟐ **5. Reflect and Adjust**

Each day, write one thing that worked and one tweak to try next.

Power Quote:

"The only way to build an AI-powered future is to start now—with curiosity, courage, and a willingness to learn."

— David Moore

About the Author

David Moore is a seasoned author, known for his intricate suspense thrillers that delve into the murky world of conspiracies and high-stakes drama. With a background in freelance writing, David spent years writing about political scandals and global conflicts, experiences that now fuel his gripping narratives.

www.ingramcontent.com/pod-product-compliance
Lightning Source LLC
LaVergne TN
LVHW090321210926
848480LV00001B/321
* 9 7 9 8 2 3 1 4 3 6 8 0 4 *

MOSFET CIRCUITS GUIDEBOOK–
with 100 Tested Projects

Other TAB books by Rufus P. Turner

Book No.	63	Transistor Circuits
Book No.	69	Electronic Hobbyist's Handbook
Book No.	75	Transistors—Theory & Practice
Book No.	537	125 One-Transistor Projects